# GO GRAMMAR! 4

## A HOMEWORK AND IN-CLASS WORKBOOK



EDITION 3

L DERIU • P GARLICK

Go Grammar! 4
3rd Edition
Laura Deriu
Pam Garlick

Publishing editor: Michael Spurr
Project editor: Mandy Herbet
Editor: Carolyn Glascodine
Proofreader: Sarah Blood
Permissions researcher: Debbie Gallagher
Cover design: Leigh Ashforth, Watershed Design
Text design: Leigh Ashforth, Watershed Design
Cover image: Canine Feline by Fin DAC. Alamy Stock Photo/Steve Vidler
Production controller: Erin Dowling
Typeset by: SPi Global



For product information and technology assistance,
in Australia call **1300 790 853;**
in New Zealand call **0800 449 725**

For permission to use material from this text or product, please email **aust.permissions@cengage.com**

ISBN 978 0 17 038953 2

**Cengage Learning Australia**
Level 7, 80 Dorcas Street
South Melbourne, Victoria Australia 3205

**Cengage Learning New Zealand**
Unit 4B Rosedale Office Park
331 Rosedale Road, Albany, North Shore 0632, NZ

For learning solutions, visit **cengage.com.au**

Printed in Malaysia by Papercraft.
6 7 8 9 24

# CONTENTS

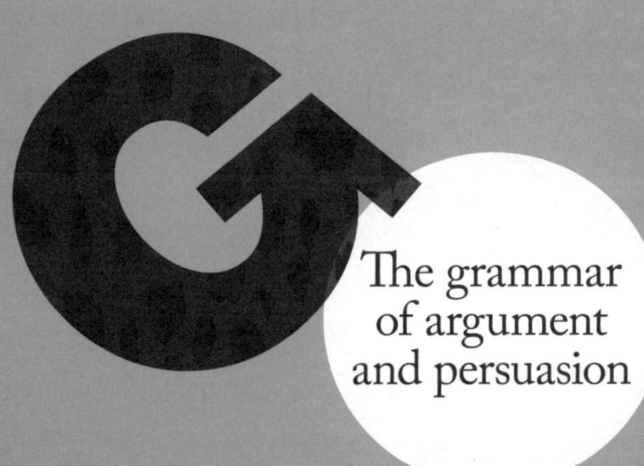

## The grammar of reading, writing and viewing texts



## The grammar of responding to texts

# INTRODUCTION

The *Go Grammar!* series focuses on the language conventions of English: its grammar, spelling, punctuation, vocabulary and usage. This book uses the metalanguage of English – technical words such as 'preposition', 'clause', 'simile' or 'suffix' – that you need to know in order to discuss the way language is used in your writing, reading and viewing, and your speaking and listening.

This edition of *Go Grammar!* includes the terms and concepts that are covered in the Australian Curriculum: English.

In *Go Grammar 4* students are also introduced to a broad range of writing techniques and text types. These sections of the book enable students to apply their understanding of language conventions to creating and interpreting texts. These skills will help lay a solid foundation for senior English subjects.

Some concepts and exercises in this book will be familiar to you. You will be able to work through some sections quickly, revising material that you have encountered. Other sections will be new to you, and you need to be quite sure that you understand each new concept before moving on to the next unit. Ask your teacher to provide exercises for extra practice if you think you need them.

Mastering these units of work will make you a better writer, reader, viewer, speaker and listener. It will also assist you in facing tests with more confidence.

Each unit is organised into three sections:

**EXPLANATION**:
You will find this box at the beginning of each unit. Sometimes there is a second explanation box later in the unit, to teach you another part of the topic. Memorise these sections.

**HAVE A GO** exercises:
These exercises allow you to practise what you have read and memorised in the explanation. For example, you might need to show that you can identify a part of speech or that you can correctly punctuate a sentence.

**TAKE IT FURTHER** exercises:
These exercises are usually more challenging, allowing you to check that you really understand the topic.

You will also find in this book:

**REVISION TEST**: Use this test to make sure that you have understood the work you have done in the preceding units.

**SPELLING FOCUS** sections:
Many units in *Go Grammar! 4* include Spelling Focus activities. Use these exercises to consolidate your knowledge English spelling.

Answers to all the exercises in this book are available for your teacher. When there is more than one possible response, we suggest that you work with a partner to check each other's answers. Working with a partner is a good way of making sure that you have understood every topic.

We hope you enjoy working through the exercises in this book and discover new and interesting things about grammar.

# AUTHOR ACKNOWLEDGEMENTS

Much gratitude to my teaching colleagues and students, and the editorial team; as well as Karen, Harry, Nina and Tara.

Laura Deriu

This is dedicated to the many students from whom I have learnt so much over the years, and to Bez, David and James who are so supportive of all my work.

Pam Garlick

Name: | Due date: | Guardian signature:

# 1 OVERVIEW OF PARTS OF SPEECH

Grammar, language usage and editing

## NOUNS

**Nouns** are naming words for a person, place, creature, thing, quality, idea or feeling. Nouns can be concrete (common nouns, proper nouns and collective nouns) or abstract.

 girl, house, elephant, Olympic Stadium, tribe, happiness

Nouns are usually part of a **noun group**.

 the little girl in the blue dress, the large house on the corner, an African elephant

| Part of speech | Definition | Examples | Hint |
|---|---|---|---|
| Common noun | Naming word for a person, place, creature or thing | cat, basketball, bush, boy, father | |
| Proper noun | Naming word for a particular person, place, special day, book or film title, business or organisation | Luisa Crane, Melbourne, Passover, *To Kill a Mockingbird*, Engineers Without Borders | Always begin with a capital letter |
| Collective noun | Naming word for a group or collection of people, animals or objects | team, class, staff, herd, flock | Usually followed by a singular verb |
| Abstract noun | Naming word for a quality, idea or feeling | kindness, thought, hatred | |

In English most nouns form their plurals by adding –s. A few require a change of spelling when the –s is added; for example:

→ nouns ending in *–y* change the *–y* to *i* before adding the *–s* (*fly–flies, trophy–trophies*) unless there is a vowel before the *y* (*valleys, essays, delays*)

→ nouns ending in *–f* and *–fe* often change the *–f* to *v* and add *–es* (*hoof–hooves, knife–knives*, but note *roof–roofs, cliff–cliffs, chief–chiefs*)

→ nouns ending in *sh* or *ch* add *–es* (*sash–sashes, beach–beaches*)

→ some nouns ending in *–o* add *–es* (*potato–potatoes, tomato–tomatoes*)

Many foreign words have now been anglicised and simply add –s or *–es*. Because they have a different plural in their source language, it is not uncommon to find the foreign plural form in English; for example:

→ *bacterium–bacteria, alumnus–alumni* (Latin)

→ *criterion–criteria, hypothesis–hypotheses* (Greek)

→ *beau–beaux, chateau–chateaux* (French)

→ *cherub–cherubim, kibbutz–kibbutzim* (Hebrew)

A small group of very common words still form their plurals as they did in Old English, such as *men, women, children, mice, feet* and *teeth*.

Nouns, verbs, adjectives and adverbs are sometimes classified as content or lexical words.

**1** Complete the table below by writing each of the underlined nouns in the correct column.

William sat on the hatch away from the crowd, listening to the cries of the crew and watching the sails fill with wind. It was to be a great adventure; perhaps the greatest adventure of all. Leaving Badsworth was difficult because they were forced to say goodbye to their families and, for him, it meant the last chance to lay some flowers on the grave. He could hardly believe that David had been dead for a decade.

| Common | Proper | Collective | Abstract |
|---|---|---|---|
| | | | |
| | | | |
| | | | |
| | | | |
| | | | |
| | | | |
| | | | |

## PRONOUNS

Pronouns are used in place of a noun. There are five different types of pronoun.

| Part of speech | Definition | Examples | Hint |
|---|---|---|---|
| Personal pronoun | Used in place of a noun to name people, animals or things | *I* wish that *you* had been able to meet *them*. | Select carefully according to case and number |
| Possessive pronoun and possessive adjective | Used to show ownership | It is *my* book. It is *mine*.<br>It is *our* garden. It is *ours*. | Don't confuse the two possessives |
| Interrogative pronoun | Asks a question | *Who* will go with me?<br>*What* is that? | |
| Reflexive pronoun | Formed by adding *–self* or *–selves* | She cut *herself* badly. | Can be used for emphasis; e.g. Peter walked the dog *himself*. |
| Relative pronoun | Relates to the noun or pronoun preceding it | The skier *who* fell was airlifted to hospital. | People: *who, whom, whose*<br>Animals, objects, things, ideas: *which, that, whose* |

**2** Underline the pronouns in the sentences below and identify their type.

**a** You should be able to do that. ______

**b** Maddie gave the money to him. ______

**c** On the oval, Carlos kicked the ball by himself. ______

**d** Who will help me? ______

## VERBS

| Part of speech | Definition | Examples | Hint |
|---|---|---|---|
| Verb (1) | Action word (usually describes physical or mental actions) | I *ate* the apple.<br>John *must go* to the football. | Select the appropriate form and tense<br>Strengthen writing by using a wide range of verbs |
| Verb (2) | Verbs of being, sensing and relating | She *is* a student.<br>She *became* a teacher.<br>I *feel* excited. | |
| Transitive verb | Has an object | The dog *shook* the bone. | Some verbs can be either transitive or intransitive |
| Intransitive verb | Doesn't have an object | The dog *shook* with excitement.<br>She *coughed* uncontrollably. | Some verbs are always either transitive or intransitive |
| Active verb | The subject of the verb is the 'doer' of the action | The trees *groaned* and *moaned* in the wind. | Some companies use active verbs to promote 'plain English' in communication with customers |
| Passive verb | The subject of the verb is the 'receiver' of the action | The trees *were lashed* by the strong winds. | Often used in formal documents (legal, scientific)<br>Sometimes used by authors to convey a character's powerlessness/lack of control |

**1** Write sentences in the second column of the table below, retaining the verbs in bold but changing the form from transitive to intransitive.

| Transitive | Intransitive |
|---|---|
| He **ran** to the shops. | |
| She **shook** the paper. | |
| Have you **eaten** all the bananas? | |

**2** Change the passive verbs to active verbs, making your sentences as direct as possible.

**a** Constructive action is being considered by the government department.

**b** Traces of whipped cream could be seen around his lips.

c Changes will be implemented by the school council.

d The news of the robbery was reported by the journalist.

## ADJECTIVES

| Part of speech | Definition | Examples |
|---|---|---|
| Adjective | Describes a noun or pronoun and adds to its meaning<br>Qualifies the noun or pronoun by describing it in terms of its shape, size, texture or colour | The box was *square*.<br>The *huge* tiger stalked its prey.<br>He rode his bike on the *smooth* paving.<br>I bought the *red* dress. |
| Comparative adjective | Used to compare one object or person with another | The horse is the *larger* of the two. That dish is *hotter* than the other. |
| Superlative adjective | Used to compare more than two objects or people | That horse is the *largest* in the race.<br>That dish is the *hottest* of all. |

## ADVERBS

| Part of speech | Definition | Examples |
|---|---|---|
| Adverb | Modifies a verb, another adverb or an adjective<br>Tells us *how* (manner), *when* (time), *where* (place) and *to what extent* (degree) | He gestured *aggressively* at the umpire.<br>I will go to the station *tomorrow*.<br>She looked *everywhere* for her friend.<br>I was *extremely* sick. |

**3** Name the parts of speech underlined in the sentences below.

a Jake is the hardest worker among the charity helpers.

b The judge insisted that the witness be more specific.

c He is the slower of the pair.

d Laura tried everywhere, shopping for the biggest tarpaulin.

Select adjectives carefully; some have no comparative or superlative degree; for example: *unique, equal, final, last, perfect.*

Name: | Due date: | Guardian signature:

# 2 PREPOSITIONS

Grammar, language usage and editing

A **preposition** shows the relationship between people, things and actions.

e.g. The pen rolled *behind* the bookcase.
The child ran *into* the garden.
The man walked *across* the bridge.

Common prepositions include:

| | | | | |
|---|---|---|---|---|
| above | beneath | in | out | under |
| across | by | into | over | up |
| before | down | like | round | upon |
| behind | during | near | through | with |
| below | from | of | to | within |

*Writing tip*: In spoken English we often finish sentences with prepositions, but we should avoid doing so in written English.

e.g. Where are you going *to*? Where are you going?
What are you doing that *for*? Why are you doing that?

Some words go together with particular prepositions. It is important to learn these 'pairs'.

e.g. When you *compare* this contract *with* the other one, it is clear which one should be signed.
George is *dedicated to* his music.
Tran's jumper was *different from* mine.

Sometimes there are quite precise distinctions in meaning according to preposition selection.

e.g. Jack *agrees with* the sports commentator.
Carly *agrees to* the deal.
He is *happy with* his pay.
She is *happy to* continue playing in that position.

Be aware of the following prepositions, which could trip you up.

e.g. He hid the CDs *between* his schoolbooks. (two things)
The skateboarder crashed *among* the spectators. (more than two things)

*Off* is the opposite of *on* and should not be used instead of *from*.

e.g. Juanita borrowed the car *off* her mother. ✗
Juanita borrowed the car *from* her mother. ✓

A preposition should not be confused with an adverb. A preposition shows the relationship between two things.

e.g. She hid *under* the railing.

An adverb modifies a verb, an adverb or an adjective and is able to stand alone.

e.g. He was swimming well and then he went *under*.

Prepositions are sometimes classified as structural words, along with pronouns, conjunctions and determiners such as *the*, *a*, *this* and *these*.

**1** Correct the following sentences.

a The arrow pierced through the target.

b The mountaineering party descended down to base camp.

c Hockey is different than lacrosse.

d Annie is dedicated about her tennis.

**1** Write as many suitable prepositions as you can think of to add to the questions below.

a The nurse was [preposition] the hospital.

b The helicopter flew [preposition] the river.

c The dog chased the cat [preposition] the garden.

**2** Make up sentences containing the following words, using appropriate prepositions.

a defend

b apologise

c grateful

d different

| Name: | Due date: | Guardian signature: |
|---|---|---|

# 3 CONJUNCTIONS AND TEXT CONNECTIVES

Grammar, language usage and editing

A **conjunction** is used to join units of language and can connect words, phrases or sentences.

e.g. He went to the ground, *but* the match had been moved.
They lit a fire on the beach *because* the sun had set.

Common conjunctions include:

| | | | | |
|---|---|---|---|---|
| after | because | however | though | where |
| although | before | if | unless | whether |
| and | but | or | until | while |
| as soon as | for | since | when | yet |

e.g. *Although* my car is old, I can't afford a new one.
Mark *and* Tyrone wrote their essays, *but* didn't submit them.

**Coordinating conjunctions** (*and*, *but*, *or*) join words or clauses of equal importance.

e.g. The plane was late *and* I missed my next connection.
I will ask him *but* he doesn't usually comment.
Choose this toy *or* choose the other one.

Conjunctions that join less important (subordinate or dependent) clauses to a main or independent clause are called **subordinating conjunctions**.

e.g. He will go to the concert *because* the band is first-rate.
James rode his bike *until* it was nearly dark.

**Relative pronouns** may also be used as link words.

e.g. The DVD, *which* I borrowed from my friend, had scratches on the playing surface.
The mechanic, *whose* wrench I borrowed, was working on my cousin's car.
Sam, *who* won the citizenship prize, has gone to Surfers Paradise.

**Text connectives** are adverbs or adverbial phrases that are used to link sentences or paragraphs. They include adverbs such as *however*, *nevertheless*, *then*, *firstly*, *finally*, *therefore*, *consequently* and adverbial phrases such as *on the other hand* and *in the first place*.

Note that text connectives are punctuated differently from conjunctions. They are usually preceded by a full stop(.) or sometimes by a semicolon(;)

e.g. I told him the truth. *However*, it was clear that he did not believe me.
I told him the truth; *on the other hand*, I neglected to include all the facts.

Coordinating conjunctions join main or independent clauses; subordinating conjunctions link subordinate or dependent clauses to other clauses.

**1** Complete the sentences with appropriate conjunctions.

a I should have handed in my project today, ______________ I was given an extension.
b ______________ he was soaked on the way home, the elderly man fell ill with pneumonia.
c ______________ the exams are over, we're going on schoolies' week.
d The dog hasn't been the same ______________ the rabbit joined the household menagerie.
e You have no hope of going to the concert ______________ you bought a ticket ages ago.

## TAKE IT FURTHER

**1** Choose conjunctions from the list on page 7 to join the sentences. The first one has been done for you.

a Emus cannot fly. Emus have wings.

Although emus have wings, they cannot fly.

b You may play tennis. The court is wet.

c She is staying at the beach house. Her sister will stay away.

d The doctor was completing the operation. The lights went out.

e He will pose for the photo. He is very handsome.

**2** Underline the text connectives in the following sentences and then rewrite the sentences, punctuating them correctly using a full stop or a semicolon.

a I accepted the invitation, however I don't expect to stay long.

b He showed me how to make the model firstly he helped me cut out the wood.

The sentence order to best convey your meaning. 'Penguins cannot fly. Penguins have wings.' becomes 'Although penguins have wings, they cannot fly.'

Name: | Due date: | Guardian signature:

# 4 CLAUSES AND PHRASES

Grammar, language usage and editing

## CLAUSES

| Clause | Definition | Examples | Hint |
|---|---|---|---|
| Clause | A group of words that contains a subject and a verb | Tamara joined the rowing club, // but she couldn't swim. | Two types: main and subordinate |
| Main or independent clause | Expresses the main message of a sentence | The horses galloped across the paddock. | Usually makes complete sense on its own |
| Coordinate clause | One or more additional main clauses in a sentence | The forward scored a goal // and his teammates applauded. | Joined with conjunctions such as *and* or *but* |
| Subordinate or dependent clause | Offers extra information but cannot stand alone<br>Begins with conjunctions such as *if*, *that*, *when*, *because*; or with relative pronouns such as *who*, *whom* and *which* | *Because the fire was approaching quickly*, the firefighters withdrew to the other side of the firebreak. | Three types: noun, adjectival and adverbial |
| Noun clause | Does the work of a noun | They selected *equipment* (noun).<br>They selected *what they wanted* (noun clause). | Can be the subject or object of a verb |
| Adjectival clause | Qualifies a noun or a pronoun | He competed in the sports *at which he excelled.* | |
| Adverbial clause | Modifies a verb, adverb or adjective | They waited impatiently *while the curtain was raised.* | More than one type (see also adverbs) |

*Note:* Clauses are often embedded within other clauses, as when an adjectival clause is used to extend a noun group.

 The athletes *who had been chosen for the Olympics* tried on their new uniforms.

Write the clauses in the following sentences and identify the type of clause.

**a** There was an explosion that he had certainly not expected.

Clauses need a finite verb.

**b** As he rounded the corner, he was met by a most unusual sight.

**c** Mount Williams is a resort where water sports dominate the activities.

**d** She climbed the hill and saw an amazing sunset.

## PHRASES

| Phrase | Definition | Examples | Hint |
|---|---|---|---|
| Phrase | Unit of language that does not contain a finite verb | The medic *with the large black case* pushed towards the collapsed man. | Used in a similar way to a noun, adjective or adverb |
| Noun phrase | Stands in place of a noun | The council has banned *skating in the park*. | May be the subject or object of the verb |
| Adjectival phrase | Stands in place of an adjective | I will buy the red dress from the tailor *round the corner*. | Qualifies a noun |
| Adverbial phrase | Stands in place of an adverb | *Before next summer*, we should paint the shed. | Modifies a verb, adverb or adjective |

Write the phrases in the following sentences and identify the type of phrase.

**a** I buy paint from the hardware shop on the corner.

**b** You will see him on the corner.

**c** He hates eating red meat.

**d** The team in their national uniforms marched past.

**e** Run the electrical cable before painting the woodwork.

| Name: | Due date: | Guardian signature: |
|---|---|---|

# 5 THE SENTENCE

Grammar, language usage and editing

## LANGUAGE FEATURES

| Language feature | Definition | Example | Hint |
|---|---|---|---|
| Sentence (can be a statement, question, exclamation or command) | A unit of language complete in itself | Naomi is jogging along the river path.<br>Is Naomi jogging along the river path?<br>Naomi is jogging along the river path!<br>Naomi, jog along the river path! | Two sections: subject and predicate |
| Subject | Person or thing to whom or to which the sentence refers | The white flag was slowly raised *by the soldier.*<br>*Matt* is feeling rather unhappy about the result. | The subject is not always at the beginning of the sentence |
| Predicate | What is said or written about the subject | Thousands of people *watched the football final.*<br>English *is my favourite subject.* | Must contain a verb |

**1** Underline the subject in each sentence.

- **a** The physics assignment took two weeks to complete.
- **b** Music is enjoyed by many people around the world.
- **c** This report aims to investigate the pollution in the river.
- **d** The harbour beaches are unfit for swimming or surfing.
- **e** Climate change is a very serious problem.
- **f** The gardener dug the flower beds in the park.
- **g** The skater refused to wear a helmet.

**2** Underline the predicate in each sentence.

- **a** You are urged to support clean-up days.
- **b** The findings suggest that a greener solution is possible.
- **c** Is Taj going to the dance?
- **d** His answer is quite different from mine.
- **e** Lily could not find her gloves.
- **f** Jordi left his sister behind.
- **g** Tina was learning to drive.

**Unless you are writing a narrative, incomplete or fragmented sentences should be avoided in written texts.**

## SENTENCES

| Sentence types | Definition | Example |
|---|---|---|
| Simple sentence | Contains only one independent clause | The winner collected her prize. |
| Compound sentence | Contains two or more independent clauses | He walked to the front of the theatre, but he could not climb the steps. |
| Complex sentence | Contains a independent clause and one or more subordinate clauses | Jason needed his daily dose of chocolate to ensure prolonged concentration. |
| Compound–complex sentence | Contains at least two independent clauses and at least one subordinate clause | Evie travelled to the tennis, but she did not get the best seat because the train was delayed. |

*Note:* Incomplete sentences are a common feature of spoken language and of dialogue. While they can be used for effect in writing, they need to be treated with care, as they can give the impression of careless writing.

Identify the sentence types using the information in the table above.

**a** The basketball player was very tall. ______________________

**b** Soft-drink vending machines are profitable in schools. ______________________

**c** Although he argued against going, David enjoyed himself. ______________________

**d** Have you seen the paper I wrote on the project? ______________________

**e** The wall was reinforced, but the building fell down. ______________________

**f** A slide presentation on carbon footprints is being delivered. ______________________

**g** A special cake was baked and it was presented to the committee member who had done all the hard work. ______________________

**h** The writer returned to the house where he had lived during his teens. ______________________

**i** The child caught two fine salmon, but he put them back into the water because of the park rules. ______________________

**j** Namiko was told that the match would be late starting. ______________________

**k** The shot was hit but the ball went astray. ______________________

**l** The trophy was engraved and awarded to the team member who had sold the most merchandise. ______________________

Name: | Due date: | Guardian signature:

# 6 EDITING – CONTENT AND STRUCTURE

Grammar, language usage and editing

**Editing** is an important activity that should become an essential part of refining your work. Your purpose and audience will influence the types of editing procedures you use.

**Transactional writing**, such as that in a text/context/comparative essay, a persuasive/informative essay or a presentation, requires you to develop a logical structure that clearly scaffolds your point of view/analysis or information/argument. Editing may involve restructuring part of or an entire essay. It may also involve changing the form of your work to improve its ability to fulfil your purpose. You may decide to change from an essay, for example, to a speech or newspaper article. You should also ensure that you support your views with suitable evidence.

**Personal/imaginative writing** involves using structures that often reflect a wider range of purposes and audiences than the type of writing mentioned above. Although the content may be more personal in nature, there are still editorial decisions to be made in relation to form, structure and vocabulary to ensure the greatest success for your piece. Remember that editing is a much more complex process than simple proofreading. Proofreading deals with mechanical or technical matters such as spelling, formatting, punctuation and so on, and is only a *part* of the editing process, best completed after you have finished editing your work.

Never be afraid to make the changes that may occur to you during the editing process, even if you think it will involve extra work. Good planning and editing are essential to success in essay writing.

**1** The following process provides easily recognisable cues to allow you to check that:

- → the structure of your essay is both appropriate and clear
- → your argument is developed logically and therefore the line of argument is clear
- → discussion of major points is evident in each paragraph
- → supportive evidence is used in each paragraph
- → paragraphs are linked.

You will need different-coloured highlighters/pencils and a draft of a transactional essay that you have written. Use a different colour to highlight/underline each part of the process. The essay can come from any subject that you are studying.

**Introduction to the essay**

**a** Underline your contention/response to the question.

**b** Underline your brief background or contextualising of the subject.

**c** Highlight the major three or four points that contain your argument and which should contain your topic sentences for the body of the essay.

**Body of the essay**

**d** In each body paragraph, highlight the topic sentence.

**e** In each body paragraph, highlight the discussion/expansion of the topic sentence.

The structure of your writing depends on your audience and purpose.

f In each body paragraph, highlight the material used as supporting evidence.
g In each body paragraph, highlight the link to the next paragraph/point.

**Conclusion**

h Underline your re-statement of the contention/question.
i Highlight the major arguments you have used to discuss the topic.
j Underline your concluding/contextualising statement.

**2** For this exercise, you will need a sample of your personal writing, such as a story or a journal entry. Use highlighters to assist you in asking the following questions of your personal writing.

a What is the audience and purpose of the piece – its focus?
b What are the basic characteristics and ideas of the piece? Has anything been omitted?
c Does everything relate to the central focus of the piece?
d Is there a theme? Is it developed effectively?
e Are there words – or even sentences or paragraphs – that contribute very little to the overall impact of the piece of writing? Could the writing be improved by cutting some words or sentences?
f Does the imagery follow the rule of 'show, don't tell'? Does it dramatise your writing?
g If characters are used, how are they revealed? Are characters revealed through action or through dialogue?
h Do you need to rearrange the structure? Does it support your content? Is there a better way than the beginning–middle–end sequence?
i Is dialogue necessary? Is it convincing? Is it appropriate to your audience and purpose?

- → Form an editing group with two or three classmates. The group should be no larger than this at any time.
- → You will need a pen and paper and a good-quality draft of your latest imaginative piece.
- → Read your work aloud to the group. The other members jot down comments, questions and advice to discuss with you when you have finished reading your draft.
- → Take these discussions seriously; though, of course, you do not have to follow the suggestions made by your group.
- → Make a note of any comments/suggestions that you want to consider when preparing your final draft.
- → Write a revised draft.
- → If necessary, check again with your editing group to see if your changes are effective.

Name: | Due date: | Guardian signature:

# 7 EDITING – WORD CHOICE

Grammar, language usage and editing

Choosing the most effective words helps achieve accuracy, clarity and economy in conveying descriptions and ideas. The right words will reduce expression problems such as ambiguity, repetition of vocabulary, verbosity and circumlocution. Edit your **word choices** to ensure clear communication.

→ **Verbosity** is the excessive use of words – often the use of extremely formal or technical words – when a simple word would suffice.

→ **Circumlocution** involves using an excessive number of words, which results in indirect (or meandering, roundabout) expression.

→ **Redundancy** is when extra, useless or 'lazy' words are used.

→ **Tautology** is excessive repetition.

All of these word choice errors can cause confusion and boredom in the reader or listener.

Remove instances of verbosity, circumlocution, redundancy and tautology in the following sentences by applying one (or more) of the following strategies.

→ Delete words or phrases that do not contribute to the sentence (known as *redundant*).

→ Delete *qualifiers* and *modifiers* (such as 'Needless to say …'; 'In point of fact …').

→ Eliminate *self-references* (such as *I* … or *My* …).

→ Use simple or familiar words.

**a** The students read Khaled Hosseini's 340-page paperback novel *The Kite Runner*.

**b** In point of fact, we need to interact and intercommunicate – that is to say that we need to converse and correspond with each other.

**c** Providing that the product is used in accordance and compliance with the operating and usage instructions, it should work perfectly.

**d** The juvenile female and her pet, a member of the canine species, went missing from her place of residence.

Editing involves attention to word choice. Ask yourself: 'Is there a more effective word?'

**e** The law-enforcement officer suspected that the fatigued motorist had partaken of excessive alcoholic liquid, which caused him to manoeuvre his vehicle in an irregular manner.

**f** That is enough and sufficient sustenance for the party.

**1** The underlined words in the following paragraph are inadequate or repetitious. Replace them with more accurate and effective words. Then explain other changes you would make to improve the paragraphs.

Why do people have different views about the same event? Every human being is an individual and even though we might experience the same event we will each have a <u>different</u> view on it because of our individuality. The same event can be like a <u>different</u> reality for everyone involved in it because it may mean <u>different things</u> to everyone. There are so many <u>different</u> factors that influence how we <u>view things</u> and create our idea of reality. For example, the way we <u>view things</u> might be influenced by our past experiences, peer pressure, upbringing and family or even the <u>things</u> we personally like or dislike. Memory plays a part in how we <u>view things</u> because our individual recollections of events differ.

**2** Student bloopers are serious, but humorous, errors made by students in their responses. Search for 'student bloopers' on the Internet. Collect some examples. State the kind of word choice error(s). Rewrite the 'student blooper' so that it communicates clearly.

Name: | Due date: | Guardian signature:

# 8 PROOFREADING

Grammar, language usage and editing

**Proofreading** deals with the technical and mechanical aspects of writing. It is an important part of the editing process as it ensures that your work is presented in the best possible light, whether for publication, assessment or presentation. During proofreading:

- → ensure that all grammatical errors have been corrected
  - → remember that not all the features of modern speech are acceptable in written work and use of texting language is unacceptable in formal schoolwork
- → check features such as the following:
  - → verb agreement – do verbs agree with their subject in number and person?
  - → selection and placement of individual words (if in doubt, consult a dictionary)
  - → punctuation, especially apostrophes, quotations and direct speech/dialogue
  - → sentence structure – do sentences require alteration to their length, structure, organisation or placement?
  - → tense – has the appropriate tense been used and has it been used consistently (e.g. text essays are always written in the present tense)?
  - → paragraphs – are paragraphs structured and linked so that your message is clear and your argument develops logically?
  - → style – is the style appropriate and does it enhance the form and content?
  - → vocabulary – is the vocabulary appropriate to your purpose and audience?
- → check presentation and layout of your work:
  - → Is it word-processed?
  - → Should it be double-spaced?
  - → Have you left a 3-cm margin?
  - → Have you numbered and named each page?
  - → Have you used an appropriate font style and size? (The most common are Times New Roman and Arial, size 12.) Do you need to select special fonts and layouts?
  - → Is there a cover page that identifies the author and contains all the information you have been asked to give?

Rewrite the following sentences, correcting any mistakes.

**a** The use of calculators are not permitted in this examination.

**b** Australia as well as the United States were represented at the Olympics.

**c** The statue was built in memory of a war hero killed in a road accident by his friends.

Many writers like to read their work aloud when proofreading their writing.

**d** He was the most unique player in the football league.

**e** Kate is the tallest twin.

**f** Western Australia is larger than any state in Australia.

**g** Like her mother was, Amelia has been selected for the national team.

**h** Medical research is not only conducted in Australia but also in New Zealand.

**i** No school has ever or will ever implement such a policy.

## TAKE IT FURTHER

Rewrite the following sentences, correcting any mistakes.

**a** The weeds sprung up everywhere.

**b** I believe he will play good if he's given the chance.

**c** The books have been ripped and the bookcase destroyed.

**d** It looks like it is going to rain.

**e** I am moving house he said in a tired voice.

**f** Tomorrow we are going to lay on the beach all day.

**g** I will finish the painting he said and then go to the gym.

**h** James received the news that he was to be the lead actor without a smile.

| Name: | Due date: | Guardian signature: |
|---|---|---|

# 9 FORMAL LANGUAGE

Grammar, language usage and editing

**Formal English is often characterised by an adherence to conventional standard grammar, syntax and vocabulary, as well as the formality of the context in which the text operates.**

| Feature | Formal English |
|---|---|
| Parts of speech | Parts of speech are applied according to usage rules |
| Sentence construction | Compound and complex sentences<br>Complete sentences<br>Range of phrases and clauses incorporated into sentences |
| Punctuation | Exact application of full range of punctuation marks required to clarify complex sentences with several phrases and clauses |
| Words, vocabulary, spelling | Complex vocabulary derived from Greek or Latin root words<br>A preference for nominalisation in academic writing<br>Standard English spelling<br>Technical and subject-specific terminology |
| Language and style | Impersonal and professional range of tones (objective, matter-of-fact)<br>Literary effects may be used (e.g. incorporation of figures of speech)<br>Subject-specific jargon may be used |

**Examine the following formal text about restrictions on P-plate drivers. Highlight and annotate the features of grammar, syntax and vocabulary that indicate that this is a formal piece of writing. Identify the tone (see Unit 20).**

In Victoria the introduction of a Graduated Licensing System ensures that new drivers are introduced to driving progressively. Car accident statistics in the mid-2010s showed that 21% of fatal crashes in Victoria involved probationary drivers. P1 drivers are restricted from carrying more than one peer passenger (16 to 22 years). Other restrictions include a total ban on any mobile phone use by P1 drivers, including hands-free communication devices. Further, P1 drivers must have a zero blood alcohol content (BAC). These are essential requirements to develop a good driving proficiency level record to graduate from a P1 to a P2 licence.

**1** As a class, brainstorm modes of formal writing to complete the following mind map.

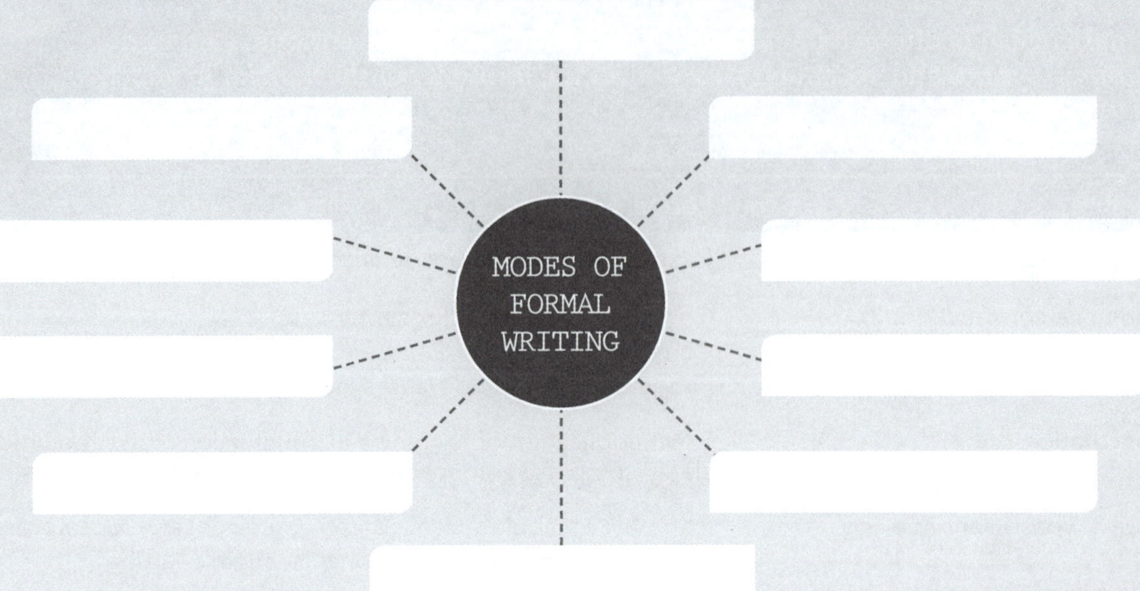


**2** As a class, undertake an excursion to the library.

**a** Find an example of a formal piece of writing in a subject area that interests you. Write the opening paragraph below.

**b** What mode of writing does the extract represent?

**c** List the features of the extract that make it a formal piece of writing.

Name: | Due date: | Guardian signature:

# 10 INFORMAL LANGUAGE

Grammar, language usage and editing

In general, the grammar, syntax, vocabulary and language usage of informal language is like that of spoken English, and occurs in more relaxed situations. Informal language is often referred to as **colloquial** or **conversational** language.

| Feature | Informal English |
|---|---|
| Parts of speech | Sentences may start with a conjunction and finish with a preposition |
| Sentence construction | Simple sentences, sentence fragments, single-word 'sentences' |
| Punctuation | Use of basic punctuation: full stops, commas, exclamation marks, question marks, apostrophes; use of dashes to reflect the structure of spoken sentences; overuse of (or idiosyncratic combination of) punctuation marks to convey emotions (e.g. *!!!* or *?!?*) |
| Words, vocabulary, spelling | Plain English vocabulary, use of vocabulary characteristic of the local region |
| Language and style | Personal, emotive and intimate range of tones and audience address; use of idioms; colloquial language; slang expressions; use of clichés; use of the conventions of spoken language; use of current 'buzzwords' |

**Idioms** are common words and expressions particular to a specific culture. **Slang** consists of highly informal words and expressions, especially as used by a particular group of people (e.g. school slang, criminal slang). A **cliché** is an expression that is so overused that its effectiveness is compromised.

**1** Below are some common Australian idioms. The meanings have been jumbled. Draw a line to match each idiom in the first column with its meaning in the second column.

| Idiom | Meaning |
|---|---|
| To choke a brown dog | To achieve success |
| To strike gold | To be completely defeated |
| To be unable to fight your way out of a paper bag | To be totally repulsive, such as inedible food |
| To be done like a dinner | To be utterly defeated or outwitted |
| To cop it sweet | To lack strength and resolve |

Informal language is mostly appropriate for spoken text.

**2** What do the following Australian slang terms mean? Do some research.

**a** To take a gander

**b** To go home in the divvy van

**c** A drongo

**d** To have Buckley's chance

**e** A tall poppy

**f** A cobber

**3** **a** Underline the clichés in the following paragraph.

Clichés are a dime a dozen. If you've seen one, you've seen them all. They've been used once too often. They've outlived their usefulness. Their familiarity breeds contempt. They make the writer look as dumb as a doormail, and they cause the reader to sleep like a log. So be as sly as a fox – avoid clichés like the plague. If you start to use one, drop it like a hot potato. Instead, be as smart as a whip. Write something that is as fresh as a daisy, as cute as a button, and as sharp as a tack. Better safe than sorry!

**b** What advice does the paragraph offer concerning the use of clichés in speaking and writing?

**TAKE IT FURTHER**

Make a list of modes of informal writing.

Name: | Due date: | Guardian signature:

# 11 NON-DISCRIMINATORY LANGUAGE

Grammar, language usage and editing

Language that expresses prejudice against people on the basis of their gender, race, religion, age, disability, culture, socioeconomic status or sexuality is considered offensive. Discriminatory language presents judgemental views of individuals and/or groups based on stereotypes and assumptions. Types of discriminatory language include sexist (on the basis of gender stereotyping and making assumptions about a person's gender), racist (on the basis of race), classist (on the basis of socioeconomic standing), ageist (on the basis of age) and heterosexist (on the basis of sexuality by assuming heterosexuality) language. The use of **non-discriminatory** language is in line with Australian democratic values and anti-harassment laws; such language ensures that people are treated equally.

Read the following sentences and explain why they are discriminatory.

**a** Mr Jack Hibbits and his little lady, Mrs Barbara Hibbits, attended the gala performance of *The Witches*. ______________

**b** It's every little girl and little boy's dream to grow up, get married and have kids.

______________

**c** Several university students, including two Muslim exchange students, were arrested for the prank. ______________

**d** The rugby players played like a pack of geriatrics! ______________

**e** Poverty among low-income earners and the unemployed is at epidemic levels due to their lack of education and tendency to gamble. ______________

**f** The accused were represented by a striking lady lawyer known for her fiery temper and high-fashion suits. ______________

**g** There were several paintings by full-blooded Aborigines on display in the gallery.

______________

**h** Although a talented surgeon, Dr Bruno Costanzo was unmarried and getting on in years.

______________

**i** 'Is he man enough to kick the winning goal?' the commentator prattled.

______________

**j** Fitness experts recommend that you should consult a doctor before embarking on a new fitness program. He will advise you on any precautions you need to take.

______________

Language should be inclusive.

The use of sexist language continues to be a problem in our society. Alter the pronouns *he*, *his* and *him* in the following sentences to make them non-discriminatory. You may be able to rewrite some of the sentences in more than one way, using the methods below.

- → rewrite the sentence in the *plural*
- → leave out the *pronoun*
- → use *he or she*, *she or he* or *s/he*
- → use *they*, *their* or *them* as gender-neutral, singular pronouns
- → rewrite the sentence using other pronouns such as *you*, *I*, *we* or *one*.

In addition, replace the word *man* with a more neutral term.

**a** Any businessman would immediately take the opportunity to expand his business customer base.

**b** An Australian Olympic sportsman trains up to 10 hours a day, seven days a week; therefore, he trains up to 70 hours per week. He usually trains at the Sports Institute or at a sports club, and he usually rides a bike or runs to training. Generally, he is on a sports scholarship; if fortunate, he may have corporate sponsorship.

**c** Before getting onto the bus, each student should check that he has his lunch, drink bottle and raincoat with him.

**d** Mankind is one of the most extraordinary species because of his ability to think in the abstract.

**e** The sausage sizzle was manned by the parents of the swimmers.

Name:

Due date:

Guardian signature:

# 12 SPELLING STRATEGIES AND 45 SPELLING DEMONS

Grammar, language usage and editing

**There are a variety of spelling strategies that you can apply.**

- → Revise the conventional spelling rules – make lists of example words for key rules. To assist with your revision, refer to units in *Go Grammar! 1, 2* and *3* that explain conventional spelling rules.
- → Say the sounds of the word aloud.
- → Create a personal spelling diary – write in all the words you find difficult to spell (double-check your spelling entries for accuracy).
- → Look for letter patterns in words – highlight/underline/circle these so that you remember them.
- → Memorise the spelling of words.
- → Create mnemonic devices to help you remember word spellings.
- → Link the spelling of a new word to a similar word you already know.
- → Use new words in your writing and conversation, paying attention to their spelling.
- → Find out the meaning of a new word – look it up, and check other spelling forms of the new word when you do so.
- → Break words into syllables, root words, suffixes and prefixes so that you become conscious of their spelling.
- → Make a sentence in which the first letter of each word can be used to make the spelling of a word.
- → Highlight/underline/circle the difficult part of the word so that you remember it.
- → Create a glossary of spelling words for your subjects, texts and so on.
- → Make up a rhyme about the spelling of a word.
- → Look at the word, note difficult parts and say the word aloud. Close your eyes and try to 'see' it. Cover the word. Write the word, saying it as you write it. Check the word letter by letter to see if you have written it correctly. Pay attention to any mistakes. Rewrite the whole word correctly a few times to reinforce it in your memory.
- → Look for words within words.
- → Exaggerate the pronunciation of words to help you recall the sequence of letters.

**1** This is a list of 25 commonly misspelt words. Practise applying one or more of the strategies listed in the explanation box above. In pairs, test each other's spelling.

| | | | | |
|---|---|---|---|---|
| weird | separate | schedule | sacrifice | receipt |
| privilege | prejudice | persuade | parallel | omission |
| occasionally | nuisance | mischievous | manageable | maintenance |
| license | liable | initiative | idiosyncrasy | hypocrisy |
| vulnerable | unconscious | unanimous | thorough | |

**2** For each word you spelt incorrectly in exercise 1, write it below, or in your workbook, in a sentence to help you practise its spelling and understand its meaning.

Keep a personal list of words that you have trouble spelling.

**1** This is a list of a further 20 commonly misspelt words. Practise applying one or more of the strategies listed in the explanation box so that you are confident with their spelling.

| | | | | |
|---|---|---|---|---|
| harassment | grievous | fluorescent | fascinate | government |
| gauge | environment | embarrassment | disastrous | descendant |
| definitely | deceive | conscientious | committee | characteristic |
| bureaucracy | approximately | amateur | accommodate | weight |

**a** Which spelling strategy(ies) did you use? List them in the space below and describe how you used them.

**b** Select two or three words from the lists above and incorporate them into one meaningful sentence.

> e.g. A *committee* was formed by the *government* to supervise the selection of *amateur* athletes.

**2** From a course textbook, select five to ten words that you find difficult to spell. List them in the space below.

**3** From a class novel that you have studied, select five to ten words that you find difficult to spell. List them below.

| Name: | Due date: | Guardian signature: |
|---|---|---|

# 13 HOMOPHONES

Grammar, language usage and editing

**Homophones** are words that sound the same, but are spelt differently and convey different meanings. The incorrect spelling of homophones is the most common of all spelling mistakes, as they cannot be detected by a computer spell-checker.

Below is a list of commonly confused homophones. Review the list and ensure that you understand the meaning of each word.

| | |
|---|---|
| air / heir | hour / our |
| aisle / isle | insight / incite |
| awe / oar / or / ore | knew / new |
| band / banned | knight / night |
| been / bean | know / no |
| bored / board | leak / leek |
| born / borne | loan / lone |
| brake / break | main / mane |
| canvass / canvas | martial / marshal |
| cell / sell | mayor / mare |
| compliment / complement | mourning / morning |
| councillor / counsellor | one / won |
| creak / creek | pair / pear |
| current / currant | pause / paws / pores / pours |
| dew / due | pray / prey |
| dissent / descent | profit / prophet |
| dual / duel | rein / reign / rain |
| earn / urn | right / wright / rite / write |
| eye / I / aye | ring / wring |
| faint / feint | road / rode / rowed |
| farther / father | sauce / source |
| faze / phase | seem / seam |
| feat / feet | sole / soul |
| for / four / fore | son / sun |
| formally / formerly | stair / stare |
| fort / fought | straight / strait |
| foul / fowl | sure / shore |
| gait / gate | taught / tort / taut |
| gorilla / guerrilla | tire / tyre |
| great / grate | vain / vane / vein |
| hail / hale | warn / worn |
| heal / heel | wave / waive |
| him / hymn | who's / whose |
| horde / hoard | wrapped / rapt |
| horse / hoarse | yolk / yoke |

Underline the correct homophone in brackets in the following news items.

### EXTRACT A

Residents of Bale woke this [mourning / morning] to discover that their local [creak / creek] had burst its banks after a [night / knight] of heavy [reign / rain / rein]. Many tried in vain to [shore / sure] up the banks. 'It was like a small [wave / waive] rolling down the [rode / road / rowed],' said one local.

### EXTRACT B

Country train commuters are seeing [red / read] over ongoing train delays, claiming that some services have been late by up to an [our / hour]. 'The [current / currant] situation cannot continue,' said [Counsellor / Councillor] Greta Sharp. 'It would [seam / seem] that the Public Transport [Board / Bored] is ignoring our [please / pleas].'

### EXTRACT C

Police made [there / their / they're] [presence / presents] obvious at a recent protest against the state government. 'We don't expect a [scene / seen],' said Constable Perkins, 'but we want to [warn / worn] people that if they choose to [brake / break] the law they will be [formerly / formally] dealt with.'

## TAKE IT FURTHER

**1** Write five sentences showing the correct usage of some homophones from the box at the beginning of the unit. Try to incorporate two or more homophones per sentence.

**2** **Research task:** People often get confused about homophones and homonyms. What is a homonym? Give some examples.

Name: | Due date: | Guardian signature:

# 14 PUBLISHING CONVENTIONS

Grammar, language usage and editing

**Whether your manuscript is handwritten or word-processed, there are basic conventions to follow if you wish to present your work professionally for grading or publishing.**

- → If you are word processing, you italicise whatever you would underline in a handwritten document (such as the title of a book or newspaper, though not the title of a poem or short story – use quote marks for these).
- → In word-processed documents, new paragraphs begin flush with the left-hand margin, with a line space above them. In handwritten versions, paragraphs are usually marked by an indentation of 1 to 2 centimetres on the first line.
- → When handwriting a document, you have an obligation to your reader to ensure that your writing is legible. In word processing, it is important to make considered decisions about the type and size of font.
- → When preparing text for a visual presentation, it is important to consider carefully the size and font in combination with templates and colour schemes.
- → It is important to acknowledge the use of another author's or speaker's material. Short quotations of single words or one or two lines should be included in the body of your writing and indicated by quotation marks. Longer quotations should be set on a new line and indented; quotation marks are not used.
- → If you are using only part of a quotation, you need to use three dots (an ellipsis) to indicate where words have been omitted.
- → If you need to add anything to a quotation (it is sometimes necessary to add something so that the meaning is clear), you should use square brackets.

*e.g.* He thought that 'the incident occurred because [he] was extremely sick.'

- → When quoting lines of verse, a forward slash is used to indicate the end of a line.

*e.g.* 'I am in blood / Stepped in so far ...'

**1** Here is a quotation from Shakespeare's *Romeo and Juliet*. The words are spoken by Friar Laurence.

These violent delights have violent ends
And in their triumph die, like fire and powder,
Which, as they kiss, consume.

A student has used this quotation in her essay. Rewrite and punctuate correctly what she wrote.

Friar Laurence is concerned about the violence of the lovers' passion and predicts a tragic outcome, using the image of fire and powder which as they kiss consume.

**Observing publishing conventions is a matter of etiquette, showing that you respect your audience.**

**2** A student wanted to quote the four lines that Romeo speaks when he first speaks to Juliet. Which of these two ways of setting out the quotation is better, **a** or **b**? ________

**a** Romeo takes Juliet's hand and says: 'If I profane with my unworthiest hand / This holy shrine, the gentle sin is this, / My lips, two blushing pilgrims, ready stand / To smooth that rough touch with a tender kiss.'

**b** Romeo takes Juliet's hand and says:

If I profane with my unworthiest hand
This holy shrine, the gentle sin is this,
My lips, two blushing pilgrims, ready stand
To smooth that rough touch with a tender kiss.

**3** In the sentences below, underline the words that would be in italics in printed text.

**a** Popular novels about young teenagers include Ruth Park's Playing Beatie Bow and Katherine Paterson's Bridge to Terabithia.

**b** 'The Loaded Dog' is probably the funniest story in Henry Lawson's short story collection Joe Wilson and his Mates.

Just as it is important to place any quoted material in quotation marks, it is essential to acknowledge all sources that you use, including electronic sources. Failing to do this is called plagiarism – the theft of another person's work or ideas. There are various ways of acknowledging quoted material. You might make an acknowledgement in the text itself (usually in brackets), and include a list of references with full publication details of your sources; or you might use footnotes. In addition, you might also include a bibliography, with a list of publications used for research but not directly quoted.

There are very precise rules for how to set out references, including the order in which the information should be listed (such as author's surname and first name, title, date of publication, place of publication, publisher, page references) and the correct punctuation. There are two main points to remember:

→ Make sure you know the referencing conventions required within the organisation for which you are writing.

→ Make sure that everything you have borrowed from anyone else is acknowledged.

**1** Find out whether your school has a policy document about referencing conventions. If it does, go through it point by point with a small group of classmates and make sure you understand it thoroughly.

**2** There is an official Australian Government guide to publishing conventions called *Style manual: for authors, editors and printers*. Find a copy in your school or local library and look up the section on referencing.

**3** Find out about Harvard referencing. You will find guides on the Internet to assist you with this system, which is used worldwide.

| Name: | Due date: | Guardian signature: |
|---|---|---|

# 15 ARGUMENT AND PERSUASION

The grammar of argument and persuasion

An **argument** is a statement (or series of related statements) that presents an **opinion** (see Unit 16) on a particular matter with the intention of **persuading** others. An argument conveys a **point of view** – that is, a statement for or against a particular matter. An argument may also be defined as a **reason** (or series of reasons) for a particular point of view.

There may be many differing and opposing arguments about controversial matters of public concern. An ongoing public debate in Australia that has provoked a range of arguments is whether voluntary euthanasia should be legalised. Some terminally ill patients and their advocates argue that voluntary euthanasia is a choice and that they have a right to die with dignity. Religious organisations and ethicists argue the sanctity of human life and draw on one of the Ten Commandments, 'Thou shalt not kill', or emphasise the spiritual value of all lives. On the other hand, doctors argue the contradictions between their obligation to alleviate suffering and the demands of their professional code called 'The Hippocratic Oath', to preserve life.

Argument styles may be described as objective or subjective.

## OBJECTIVE ARGUMENT

An **objective argument** is based on facts (see Unit 16) rather than personal opinion. This style of argument often sounds **formal** (see Unit 9). The tone is likely to be impersonal and professional, and complex sentences are common. Paragraphs are reasonably long. Nominalisation and the use of abstract nouns are characteristic features. Technical and subject-specific words are used.

## SUBJECTIVE ARGUMENT

A **subjective argument** reflects personal feelings and opinions. This style of argument usually sounds **informal** (see Unit 10). Simple sentences are common and fragmented sentences may be used. Language is colloquial, including the use of contractions such as *can't* or *won't*. Word choice favours words with emotive connotations.

## CONSTRUCTING ARGUMENT

A common type of argument structure is the **cause-and-effect** argument. This type of argument structure suggests that one factor leads directly to a specific outcome – that is there is a direct relationship between cause and effect. It can be effective if it is supported by **evidence** (see Unit 16). The writer must take into consideration all of the possible causes behind a particular effect. Text connectives used to link sentences and paragraphs include words and phrases such as *consequently*, *therefore*, *as a result* and *for this reason*.

An example of a cause-and-effect argument involves the Australian road toll. Traditionally, the Easter road toll on highways in Australia has been very high. Police claim that reduced Easter road tolls in recent years are due to increased police motorbike patrols, the reduction of the speed limit to 80 kilometres per hour and the widespread presence of 'booze buses'. Hence: increased police measures on highways (cause) result in a reduction of the Easter road toll (effect).

Another type of argument is referred to as a **reason and logic argument**. This style of argument involves the development of a point of view in a sequential, step-by-step manner using evidence and reasons. The relationships between ideas are presented in order. Text connectives used to link sentences and paragraphs include words and phrases such as *firstly*, *finally*, *next* and *in the second place*. This argument structure can also be indicated by using the following sentence frame: *If … (X), then … (Y)*; or, *If … (reason), then … (logical outcome)*.

 If Australians fail to take effective sun protection measures while outdoors, then it is likely that there will be an increase in skin cancers and melanomas.

You can learn to become a more persuasive speaker or writer.

Read the following collection of letters to the editor on the issue of homeless teenagers. Each letter presents an opinion on why there has been a dramatic increase in the number of homeless teenagers in the past 20 years. For each letter:

- → underline the sentence that expresses the writer's main argument (opinion or point of view)
- → decide whether the writer is presenting a subjective or objective argument and circle your choice.

### EXTRACT 1

More than 20 years ago, the incumbent Prime Minister, Bob Hawke, promised that no child in Australia would live in poverty by 1990. However, the situation has not improved. Welfare organisations and recent studies indicate that of the 100 000 homeless Australians on any given night, 36 per cent are aged 25 or younger. It is clear that the succession of federal governments since have failed to implement a national strategy to deal with youth homelessness. Even the government initiative in the mid-1990s – called Reconnect – failed due to underfunding. It's time for the federal government to cooperate with our state governments in showing care for our marginalised youth.

Objective or subjective?

### EXTRACT 2

I left home when I was 12. My parents drank heavily and every dinner was a massive fight about who knows what. My parents didn't get along with each other, really. Sometimes there was a bit of pushing and shoving between them. There wasn't much money, so we didn't really do much as a family except watch TV together sometimes. But that would usually end up in a massive fight also. I figured that anywhere else was better than home. So, I slept on friends' couches for a few months. I did sleep in a park a few times, but I was freaked out by that. I felt pretty worthless because my parents didn't even come looking for me. Every day was just another day to try to survive. I did some things I'm not that proud of. I would like to have stayed with my family, but it wasn't for me.

Objective or subjective?

### EXTRACT 3

Homeless kids are tough kids with tough backgrounds and tough attitudes. They are tough to deal with.

Objective or subjective?

### EXTRACT 4

Homelessness support services are inadequate. A recent report said that 42 per cent of homeless adults had been homeless teenagers. The current support services offered by the government and independent groups are just insufficient. It seems pretty clear that people are condemned to a cycle of homelessness by the system.

Objective or subjective?

Read the following extract from a news article about youth homelessness. Complete the exercises that follow.

## YOUTH HOMELESSNESS IN AUSTRALIA IS COSTING US MILLIONS

Sarah Norton

New research has called for a complete reform of youth homelessness policy in Australia.

A world-first study from Australia says we could save $626 million every year by investing in early intervention for youth justice and health costs for homeless youth.

*The Cost of Youth Homelessness in Australia (CYHA)* was released on Thursday showing the need for early intervention with young homeless people in Australia.

A media release from the study – which was conducted between 2011 and 2015 – says 'the cost to society, just from increased interactions with the health and criminal justice systems for young homeless people, exceeds the total annual cost of all homelessness services across Australia for people of all ages.'

The three principle researchers from the study were Professor David Mackenzie, Professor Paul Flatau and Professor Adam Steen with funding partners The Salvation Army, Mission Australia and Anglicare.

Mission Australia CEO, Catherine Yeoman, says we shouldn't have the amount of homeless youth in Australia today that we do.

'It is unacceptable in 21st century Australia, that there are more than 44 000 children and young people homeless on any given night,' she says in a statement as a response to the report.

'[It] paints a stark picture of the cost to society of failing to support vulnerable young people who are homeless or at a high risk of homelessness.'

The findings highlight that many young people who leave home have no choice due to family violence. In these instances, early intervention is vital to minimise health risks and criminal activity.

Professor David Mackenzie, from Victoria's Swinburne University, says the study is important because of what it has managed to show through the results.

'There's a huge additional cost that we all pay because of homelessness. The total amount is at least $626 million a year, which is more than we spend on homeless services all together,' he tells SBS.

'What we're saying to the government is, maybe you ought to do cost benefit studies in the welfare area.'

The report's media release adds: 'It calls for a complete reform of youth homelessness policy in Australia, citing a number of innovative and successful 'early intervention' programs that, if rolled out nationally, would lead to millions of dollars in savings to the economy.'

It also tackles the issue of youth that are already homeless in Australia, with hopes to look at how to best get people out of their homeless situation.

'We've got to get young people out of homelessness as soon as possible, and that's harder,' Professor Mackenzie says.

It's harder to get youth out of homelessness because they aren't always able to run a household on their own. So it is necessary to find appropriate housing opportunities.

'Keeping people in education pathways for future employment is absolutely fundamental too,' Professor Mackenzie says.

In her statement, Yeoman says that as the Federal Election nears they are urging the government to consider the findings and ensure they're investing early to prevent youth homelessness.

'We know from our experience that the long-term prospects for young people who become homeless are not good – a disjointed education, lack of support network, risky drug and alcohol use and mental illness,' she says.

'It makes sense to intervene early to address the risk factors rather than waiting until a young person is already homeless.'

Norton, S 2016, 'Youth homelessness in Australia is costing us millions', SBS.com.au, viewed 29 April 2016.

**1** Is the article objective or subjective in its style of argument? Give evidence to support your decision.

**2** This article reports the views of several experts on youth homelessness – its causes, outcomes and what can be done. Some experts use a cause-and-effect argument structure, while others use a reason and logic argument structure. Give one example of each type of argument structure.

**3** Based on the information in the article, draw a flow chart of the causes and outcomes of youth homelessness in your workbook. Add two or three additional causes of youth homelessness to your flow chart.

**4** Not all events that follow each other are related as cause and effect. Review your flow chart. Tick the causes that have direct cause-and-effect relationships on homelessness; and add a question mark next to the causes that may have a cause-and-effect relationship on homelessness.

**5** What is your opinion on what should be done to prevent homelessness among youth?

## SPELLING FOCUS

The following words appear in this unit. Add a tick next to the ones that are spelt correctly and a cross next to the ones that are spelt incorrectly. Write the correct spelling in the space next to the words spelt incorrectly.

| Word | | Correction | Word | | Correction |
|---|---|---|---|---|---|
| oppinian | [ ] | | personal | [ ] | |
| homelessness | [ ] | | benifit | [ ] | |
| objictive | [ ] | | subjictive | [ ] | |
| intervention | [ ] | | opportunities | [ ] | |

Name: | Due date: | Guardian signature:

# 16 OPINIONS, FACTS AND EVIDENCE

The grammar of argument and persuasion

When presenting an argument, individuals often aim to persuade others by presenting opinions and facts about a particular matter.

An **opinion** is an individual attitude, belief or point of view **for** or **against** a particular matter. An opinion is a personal statement about something that may have occurred or may be true, but could be open to disagreement.

A **fact** is a concrete reality; it is proven or known to have occurred. Facts can be supported by hard evidence – they can be measured in some way.

Facts often appear as **evidence** in support of an opinion. There are several types of useful evidence. These include:

→ **Personal experiences:** direct personal experiences, observations and knowledge. Personal experiences/observations are often told as anecdotes (brief stories)

→ **Definitions:** widely accepted descriptions and explanations of the meaning(s) of a concept. General dictionaries such as the *Macquarie* or *Collins*, or specialist dictionaries such as the *Dictionary of Medical Terms* or *Dictionary of Art and Artists*, can be useful

→ **Reference sources:** relevant and reliable scholarly sources such as an encyclopaedia or specialist text (including electronic sources)

→ **Statistics:** figures that show the occurrence of an event or the relationship between two events – for example, figures showing the occurrence of days with a temperature of 45 degrees over the past 10 years

→ **Polls/surveys:** 'sample opinions' whereby a small, diverse group of people (or a homogenous group of people) are questioned about their opinion on a matter. The sample opinion is taken as a general indicator

→ **Experts:** specialists with particular knowledge, experience and skill in a specific area. There are several types of experts: specialists, public figures, institutions and organisations, and eyewitnesses.

**1** Below is a list of facts and opinions about the consumption of alcohol by teenagers.

- Identify the statements of opinion by writing *O* at the end of the sentence.
- Identify the statements of fact by writing *F* at the end of the sentence.

**a** Around 73 per cent of Australian teenagers have tried alcohol at least once. ________

**b** Most teenagers drink alcohol because they are rebellious. ________

**c** The public behaviour of drunken sports stars and film stars is responsible for the dramatic upsurge of teenage binge drinking in recent years. ________

**d** Binge drinking, according to the National Health and Medical Research Council, 'is defined in most studies as six standard drinks on a single occasion.' ________

**e** Australians have a tolerant attitude towards alcohol consumption. ________

**f** Of the 27 young drivers who died in 2015, 67 per cent lost their lives in crashes that occurred during high-alcohol times such as the weekend. ________

**g** Long-term binge drinking can lead to alcohol-related brain disorders. ________

**Be alert to texts that present opinions as facts.**

**2** Are the following sentences about teenagers and the road toll fact or opinion? Write *fact* or *opinion* after each sentence and explain your answer.

**a** Motor vehicle organisations, such as the NRMA and RACV, have recorded that deaths due to road crashes are higher in the 17–24 age group than any other age group.

**b** Overconfident, risk-taking and silly teen drivers with a poor attitude are more of a menace on the roads than other motorists who drive a few kilometres over the speed limit.

**c** The new driver training regulations have led to improved driving behaviours and decreased road tolls for teen drivers.

Read the following article about teenagers and work. It includes a combination of facts and opinions. Complete the exercises that follow.

## TEENS STRESSED ABOUT STUDY AND JOBS: MISSION AUSTRALIA REPORT

Rachel Browne

Sydney's Gen Y gloomier than peers in other global cities about finding jobs

Young people are worried about high tertiary education fees and their chances of securing a job, according to a national study of Australian teenagers, which found they are increasingly doubtful about their future.

Teens are concerned about high tertiary education fees and their chances of finding a job.

Mission Australia's annual youth survey of almost 20 000 people aged 15–19 identified a decline in the proportion of youngsters feeling positive about their prospects.

Just over half the respondents felt they would face difficulty achieving their work and study goals, citing lack of jobs, financial pressure and academic ability.

Mission Australia chief executive, Catherine Yeomans, said governments and industry need to work together to provide more support for young people as they grapple with post-school options.

'These young people are not growing up in a vacuum,' she said.

'They have sisters and brothers who are not finding it easy to get a job, no matter how well they did at school, no matter how well they have done at university. They are well aware of the high rates of youth unemployment.'

It takes the average young person five years to find a full-time job after study, compared with only one year in 1986, according a report from the Foundation for Young Australians.

Competition for low-skilled work is intense, with the Department of Employment finding that an average of 18 people apply for each position.

Adding to the pressure on young people is the cost of undertaking further study to increase their chances of employment.

'Young people notice that their families are doing it tough - there is not a lot of spare cash around,' Ms Yeomans said.

'A lot of young people see others doing the courses, incurring the student debts. Young people are seeing people ahead of them who are not securing the jobs and have this sizeable debt. The return on investment comes into question.'

Coping with stress was the top issue of personal concern among the young people surveyed with young women three times more likely to say they were 'extremely concerned' about coping with stress than young men.

Ms Yeomans said that was indicative of the strains facing young people in the last few years of school, with nearly two-thirds saying they hoped to go to university after finishing year 12.

Collaroy Plateau student Danielle Wheeler, 15, hopes to study early childhood education when she finishes school and agreed there was pressure to achieve a certain ATAR.

'There is pressure to get the right score because if you don't get it you have to go through a different pathway to be accepted into the course you want and that sets you back with your degree,' she said.

Her friend Gabbi Marsh, also 15, hopes to study physiotherapy after school and was conscious of the work that lies ahead.

'If you want to get a really high ATAR you have to work hard for it,' she said. 'You can't just bludge around. You need to have a study routine. If you have a plan, it makes it less stressful because you don't leave things to the last minute.'

Browne, R 2015, 'Teens stressed about study and jobs: Mission Australia report', *Sydney Morning Herald*, 30 November 2015.

**1** Write examples of the following from the article.

**a** A statement of opinion: ______

**b** A personal experience/anecdote: ______

**c** A reference source: ______

**d** Statistics: ______

**e** A poll or survey: ______

**f** An expert opinion/advice: ______

**g** An eyewitness opinion/advice: ______

**2** Which type of evidence is the most convincing? Why?

**3** Which type of evidence is the least convincing? Why?

**4** Given the information in this unit, and your own observations, what are your opinions on teenage binge drinking, teenage drivers, and teenagers and work? Support your opinion with facts and evidence.

**5** There are many issues concerning teenagers. Choose one of the following three topics and complete tasks **a**–**d** to present and support your opinion on the topic. You will need to undertake some research.

- Schoolies' week celebrations should be banned in Australia.
- Teenage workers should be paid adult wages.
- Teenagers should not have to pay adult fares or admission prices until they are 18 years old.

**a** Chosen topic: ______________________

**b** My statement of opinion: ______________________

**c** A definition relevant to the topic: ______________________

**d** Three different types of evidence to support my statement of opinion:

**SPELLING FOCUS**

The following words appear in this unit. Add a tick next to the ones that are spelt correctly and a cross next to the ones that are spelt incorrectly. Write the correct spelling in the space next to the words spelt incorrectly.

| | | | | | |
|---|---|---|---|---|---|
| arguement | [ ] | | dissagreement | [ ] | |
| statistics | [ ] | | knowledge | [ ] | |
| proportion | [ ] | | conshious | [ ] | |
| consumtion | [ ] | | investment | [ ] | |

Name: | Due date: | Guardian signature:

# 17 EMOTIVE LANGUAGE

The grammar of argument and persuasion

**Emotive language** includes words and phrases with strong positive or negative overtones. Such language conveys approval or disapproval, and whether the writer or speaker views the matter favourably or unfavourably. Writers and speakers incorporate emotive language in order to present a convincing opinion.

Emotive language may express **bias** – that is, a one-sided opinion. On the other hand, some language may be **neutral** – that is, words or phrases that do not express bias but are impartial. For example, we use a range of words and phrases to refer to something that is *old* (neutral word). Some positive words for *old* include *antique* and *ancient*; negative words include *obsolete* and *outdated*.

Emotive language often carries **connotations** – that is, suggested meanings, ideas or associations. Connotations also express approval or disapproval. For example, the word *old-fashioned* carries negative associations that may provoke disapproval.

By incorporating emotive language into their texts, writers and speakers aim to evoke certain feelings and emotions in their audience about a topic or issue.

**1** The exercises in this unit are based on the following speech extracts. Read these speech extracts.

This speech by Stan Grant was delivered as part of the IQ2 debates (2015) on the topic: 'Racism is destroying the Australian Dream'. Grant is an Indigenous Australian reporter and social/political commentator. He started his speech by acknowledging respect for his 'Gadigal brothers and sisters from my people, the Wiradjuri people'. The opening section of the speech made reference to the racist treatment of Indigenous footballer and Australian of the Year (2014), Adam Goodes.

### EXTRACT 1

#### THE AUSTRALIAN DREAM

We sing of it, and we recite it in verse. *Australians all, let us rejoice for we are young and free.*

My people *die young* in this country. We die ten years younger than average Australians and we are far from free. We are fewer than 3 per cent of the Australian population and yet we are 25 per cent, a quarter of those Australians locked up in our prisons; and if you are a juvenile, it is worse, it is 50 per cent. An Indigenous child is more likely to be locked up in prison than they are to finish high school.

*I love a sunburned country, a land of sweeping plains, of rugged mountain ranges.*

It reminds me that my people were killed on those plains. We were shot on those plains; disease ravaged us on those plains.

I come from those plains. I come from a people west of the Blue Mountains, the Wiradjuri people, where in the 1820s, the soldiers and settlers waged a war of extermination against my people. Yes, a war of extermination! That was the language used at the time. Go to the *Sydney*

**The connotations of words allow us to make fine distinctions in meaning.**

*Gazette* and look it up and read about it. Martial law was declared and my people could be shot on sight. Those rugged mountain ranges, my people, women and children were herded over those ranges to their deaths.

The Australian Dream.

The Australian Dream is rooted in racism. It is the very foundation of the dream. It is there at the birth of the nation. It is there in *terra nullius*. An empty land. A land for the taking. Sixty thousand years of occupation. A people who made the first seafaring journey in the history of mankind. A people of law, a people of lore, a people of music and art and dance and politics. None of it mattered because our rights were extinguished, because we were not here according to British law.

And when British people looked at us, they saw something sub-human, and if we were human at all, we occupied the lowest rung on civilisation's ladder. We were fly-blown, Stone Age savages and that was the language that was used. Charles Dickens, the great writer of the age, when referring to the noble savage among whom we were counted, said 'it would be better that they be wiped off the face of the earth.' Captain Arthur Phillip, a man of enlightenment, a man who was instructed to make peace with the so-called natives in a matter of years, was sending out raiding parties with the instruction, 'Bring back the severed heads of the black troublemakers.'

Grant, S 2015, IQ2 debates 'Racism is destroying the Australian Dream'.

## EXTRACT 2

In 1963 when I was born, I was counted among the flora and fauna, not among the citizens of this country.

Now, you will hear things tonight. You will hear people say, 'But you've done well.' Yes, I have and I'm proud of it and why have I done well? I've done well because of who has come before me. My father who lost the tips of three fingers working in sawmills to put food on our table because he was denied an education. My grandfather who served to fight wars for this country when he was not yet a citizen and came back to a segregated land where he couldn't even share a drink with his digger mates in the pub because he was black.

My great grandfather, who was jailed for speaking his language to his grandson (my father). Jailed for it! My grandfather on my mother's side who married a white woman who reached out to Australia, lived on the fringes of town until the police came, put a gun to his head, bulldozed his tin humpy and ran over the graves of the three children he buried there.

That's the Australian Dream. I have succeeded in spite of the Australian Dream, not because of it, and I've succeeded because of those people.

You might hear tonight, 'But you have white blood in you'. And if the white blood in me was here tonight, my grandmother, she would tell you of how she was turned away from a hospital giving birth to her first child because she was giving birth to the child of a black person.

The Australian Dream.

We're better than this. I have seen the worst of the world as a reporter. I spent a decade in war zones from Iraq to Afghanistan, and Pakistan. We are an extraordinary country. We are in so many respects the envy of the world. If I was sitting here where my friends are tonight, I would be arguing passionately for this country. But I stand here with my ancestors, and the view looks very different from where I stand.

The Australian Dream.

We have our heroes. Albert Namatjira painted the soul of this nation. Vincent Lingiari put his hand out for Gough Whitlam to pour the sand of his country through his fingers and say,

'This is my country.' Cathy Freeman lit the torch of the Olympic Games. But every time we are lured into the light, we are mugged by the darkness of this country's history. Of course racism is killing the Australian Dream. It is self-evident that it's killing the Australian Dream. But we are better than that.

The people who stood up and supported Adam Goodes and said, 'No more,' they are better than that. The people who marched across the bridge for reconciliation, they are better than that. The people who supported Kevin Rudd when he said sorry to the Stolen Generations, they are better than that. My children and their non-Indigenous friends are better than that. My wife who is not Indigenous is better than that.

And one day, I want to stand here and be able to say as proudly and sing as loudly as anyone else in this room, Australians *all*, let us rejoice.

Thank you.

Grant, S 2015, IQ2 debates 'Racism is destroying the Australian Dream'

**a** **The extract is powerful not only because of the shocking historical facts referenced, but also because of the emotive words/phrases used throughout. Circle the positive emotive words/phrases; underline the negative emotive words/phrases.**

**b** What is the balance of positive and negative words/phrases?

**1** What event(s) provided the basis for the Stan Grant's speech?

**2** Copy out the sentence that expresses Stan Grant's main opinion.

**3** List the reasons Stan Grant gives to support his main opinion.

**4** Stan Grant repeats particular words/phrases throughout his speech. Write them out. What feelings do we associate with these words?

**5** List the emotive words/phrases that Stan Grant uses to describe the experiences of Indigenous Australians under past government laws.

**6** Do these emotive words/phrases express positive or negative overtones?

**7** What feelings and thoughts might these emotive words/phrases provoke in the audience?

**8** List the emotive words/phrases that Stan Grant uses to express hopes for the future.

**9** Do these emotive words/phrases express positive or negative overtones?

**10** What feelings and thoughts might these emotive words/phrases provoke in the audience?

**11** Find words/phrases that refer to the genocide of Indigenous Australians.

**12** What feelings and thoughts might the phrase 'genocide of Indigenous Australians' provoke?

**SPELLING FOCUS**

The following words appear in this unit. Add a tick next to the ones that are spelt correctly and a cross next to the ones that are spelt incorrectly. Write the correct spelling of the words spelt incorrectly.

| | | | | | |
|---|---|---|---|---|---|
| bias | [ ] | | connotations | [ ] | |
| associations | [ ] | | indigenious | [ ] | |
| obselete | [ ] | | dissaproval | [ ] | |
| referrence | [ ] | | evoke | [ ] | |

| Name: | Due date: | Guardian signature: |
|---|---|---|

# 18 EMOTIONAL APPEALS

The grammar of argument and persuasion

**Emotional appeals** 'hook' an audience, excite their interest and play on their feelings; they engage the audience with matters of public concern. For example, governments often make emotional appeals to our financial interests by claiming that they will lower taxes if we support their re-election. Some car advertisements make emotional appeals to our desire for safety and security by highlighting special features. Speakers and writers use a range of appeals to evoke a concerned and emotional response in their audience. Below is a list of common emotional appeals that appear in the news media and advertising.

| Emotional appeal to our ... | Description |
|---|---|
| Fears | Fears about change, danger, the unknown |
| Family values | Concerns about parents, children, threats to the sanctity of the family unit, love |
| Sense of justice | Concerns that crime is addressed and law and order are upheld |
| Sense of equality | Concerns about fairness; a 'fair go' for all |
| Morals and ethics | Concerns about upholding rights, and principled and decent behaviours; fears of immorality |
| Sense of tradition (and custom) | Concerns about maintaining past conventions, and respecting history and heritage; feelings of nostalgia for 'the good old days' |
| Patriotism | Feelings of pride in one's country |
| Tendency to conformity | Concerns about desires to 'fit in' and belong to a group or society; fears of alienation |
| Community values | Concerns about the welfare of our immediate community |
| Self-interest | Concerns about looking after our own personal interests and concerns |
| Financial concerns (hip-pocket nerve) | Concerns about threats to our financial situation, greed, materialism |
| Aspirations to be modern | Concerns about wanting to be 'cool' and up-to-date; fears of being labelled 'old-fashioned'; desires to maintain an acceptable social status |
| Sense of freedom, liberty and democracy | Concerns about protecting our individual rights under a democracy and the UN Universal Declaration of Human Rights |
| Desire for security | Concerns about our safety; fears of personal threats |
| Environmental values | Concerns about the condition of our natural world and our impact on it |

Identify the emotional appeal(s) in the following phrases.

**a** Add value to your home with these unique renovation ideas.

___

Writers and speakers use emotional appeals to influence their audiences.

**b** Your life! Your adventure! Your choice!

**c** Our cars – futuristic technology right now for your driving pleasure

**d** Government vows to give working families a break in this year's budget

**e** Tasty recipes for your waistline

**f** These screen doors are shark-proof.

**g** Everyone's wearing one! Get yours today!

**h** Australian soldiers rescue earthquake victims

**i** Reduce! Reuse! Recycle!

**j** Gas leak in city building

**k** Our classic range is tried and tested.

**l** Buy Australian – your kids and mates will thank you for it.

**m** All decent citizens will support this proposal.

**n** Donate now – it is the right thing to do.

**o** Don't get left behind; make the right choice for your prosperity.

**p** The recent laws include a clause enabling police to undertake extensive surveillance on ordinary citizens without having to explain their reasons.

**1** In a newspaper or magazine, find an advertisement that has several emotional appeals. Cut out the advertisement and paste it into the space below. Annotate the advertisement by underlining the emotional appeals and labelling them. Then complete the sentences below. (Paste and annotate the advertisement in a separate workbook if there is not sufficient space below.)

**a** This advertisement provokes the viewer's interests about:

**b** This advertisement stirs up emotions in the viewer, such as:

**2** Authors of fiction texts often embed emotive appeals in their characters in order to present a strong personality and engage the reader. Sometimes, the dominant emotive appeal in the character indicates the writer's own values.

Below is a list of paired adjectives describing personality or character traits. Write the emotional appeal(s) each trait evokes.

| Character trait | Emotional appeal |
|---|---|
| Kind-hearted and benevolent | |
| Cold-blooded and barbaric | |
| Intolerant and narrow-minded | |
| Ethical and fair-minded | |
| Cooperative and sharing | |
| Conservative and nostalgic | |
| Acquisitive and materialistic | |

**3** Think about a key character in a text you have studied. What emotional appeals are embedded in that character? What do these reveal about the author's values? Make some notes in the space below and then share your thoughts with others in the class.

**SPELLING FOCUS**

The following words appear in this unit. Add a tick next to the ones that are spelt correctly and a cross next to the ones that are spelt incorrectly. Write the correct spelling in the space next to the words spelt incorrectly.

| | | | | | |
|---|---|---|---|---|---|
| sanctity | [ ] | | nostalgia | [ ] | |
| princapeld | [ ] | | behayviour | [ ] | |
| alienation | [ ] | | matirielism | [ ] | |
| democrisy | [ ] | | accpetible | [ ] | |
| equallity | [ ] | | finantial | [ ] | |

| Name: | Due date: | Guardian signature: |
|---|---|---|

# 19 GENERALISATIONS AND SENSATIONALISM

The grammar of argument and persuasion

**Generalisations** are broad statements presenting an unsupported opinion. They imply certain assumptions and reveal the writer's values and biases. A generalisation may incorporate **stereotypes** and can be identified through the use of **inclusive terms** such as *all*, *everyone* and *humankind*. Generalisations may persuade an audience because they sound authoritative, and may contain emotional appeals and language. Additionally, they may reinforce information or ideas that are generally believed to be true. Sometimes, generalisations may be effective if the key terms are defined and evidence is supplied, and if qualifiers, such as *most*, *some*, *usually* and *probably*, are used.

Writers can convey **sensational** and **dramatic** arguments by using a range of language effects.

- → **Alliteration** is the repetition of the first letter in a sequence of words. It is attention-grabbing, and can create emphasis and reinforce ideas. It often appears in headlines or titles.
- → There are positive and negative **associations.** An argument can be strongly asserted by linking it with something generally considered in a favourable light. Likewise, an argument can be debunked by linking it with something generally considered in an unfavourable light.
- → **Attacks** communicate disapproval of a person, event or idea. They discredit or degrade by suggesting the dubious nature of the 'target' or making doubtful associations. Attacks can include 'mudslinging' – that is, attacking the person and not the issue at hand. On the other hand, **praise** focuses on the positive aspects.
- → The **repetition** of words with similar meanings in a sequence is known as **cumulation**. It creates a dramatic tone, adds emphasis and reinforces an idea. For example, 'We will show them our power, might and strength!'
- → **Hyperbole** (or **exaggeration**) involves overstatement, which can be sensational, humorous and attention-grabbing.
- → **Labelling** is the use of generic labels to identify groups of people or behaviour. This relies on recognisable stereotypes and can suggest negative or positive associations. Labelling is often used to discredit or belittle.
- → The **strategic repetition** of words, phrases, images, sentence patterns, ideas and names can be very effective in advancing an argument. Repetition can achieve reinforcement, prominence, urgency and significance.

Controversy surrounded the federal government's decision to move large numbers of asylum seekers into the community on protection visas while they waited for their applications for asylum to be processed. Read the two reports about this policy on the next page, noting how they are different.

REPORT 1

### Success of new government policy

The federal government's policy of housing asylum seekers in the community on bridging visas has been an unqualified success, according to a spokesperson for one of the charities involved with helping the newcomers to settle into their new homes.

Instead of being locked up behind barbed wire in detention centres, families are housed in rented accommodation in the suburbs of our cities and provided with a basic package of goods such as a fridge, a washing machine and beds and bedding.

'We know from past experience that most of these people will be granted permission to stay in Australia,' said a lawyer who works with asylum seeker claims. 'It made no sense to lock them up in detention centres for months, with all the accompanying mental health problems, when they are going to be Australian citizens.'

**Be suspicious of texts that use sensationalism or sweeping generalisations.**

REPORT 2

## Aussie taxpayers slugged again

Hundreds of boat people have been given taxpayer-funded welcome packs to set up houses in our suburbs. The packages, administered by the Red Cross, are worth up to $10000 and include beds, fridges, mattresses, couches and even a television set with a minimum screen size of 53 cm. In all, the list contains more than 60 items. This assistance is on top of free medical and dental treatment, free prescriptions, free schooling and even free legal aid, as well as payments of up to $433.25 a fortnight. Ed McCoy, who has watched a family of five move into a house in his street, told our reporter: 'You have to come here in a rickety boat to get some semblance of service from this government. The rest of us have to slave for a loaf of bread. These freeloaders are looked after like royalty.'

**1** How are the reports different?

**2** Both reports are mostly factual. However, one of them is more likely to result in feedback denouncing the 'luxury' in which 'these illegals/queue jumpers' are living. Which report do you think might lead to such a response?

**3** What evidence is there that the second report was written to provoke an angry response?

**4** Find evidence in either report of:

**a** words chosen for their positive or negative associations

**b** exaggeration

**c** personal attacks

**d** the cumulation of details and/or repetition

**5** Write the opening paragraph of an editorial condemning the new policy, under the headline: 'Charity begins at home!' Use techniques to persuade your readers to accept your point of view.

**6** Write the opening paragraph of an editorial explaining that the new policy makes good practical sense, under the headline: 'Do we really want to condemn asylum seekers to begging on our streets?' Use techniques to persuade your readers to accept your point of view.

## TAKE IT FURTHER

Magazines reporting on the entertainment industry and sports events incorporate a variety of sensational and dramatic effects. Working with a partner, review current magazines that report on the entertainment industry or sports events. These may be online. Find and write examples of the following techniques.

**a** An attack

**b** Praise

**c** A positive association

______________________________

______________________________

**d** A negative association

______________________________

______________________________

**e** Hyperbole/exaggeration

______________________________

______________________________

**f** Labelling

______________________________

______________________________

**g** Repetition

______________________________

______________________________

**h** Stereotyping

______________________________

______________________________

**i** Identify the tone, name it and give an example.

______________________________

______________________________

## SPELLING FOCUS

The following words appear in this unit. Add a tick next to the ones that are spelt correctly and a cross next to the ones that are spelt incorrectly. Write the correct spelling in the space next to the words spelt incorrectly.

| Word | | Correction | Word | | Correction |
|---|---|---|---|---|---|
| generalisation | [ ] | | exageration | [ ] | |
| renforcments | [ ] | | sensashional | [ ] | |
| associations | [ ] | | prominence | [ ] | |
| repeatition | [ ] | | dubouse | [ ] | |

| Name: | Due date: | Guardian signature: |
|---|---|---|

# 20 TONE

The grammar of argument and persuasion

In written and spoken communication, the writer's **tone** conveys their attitudes and feelings towards the material under consideration. Tone is often referred to as 'the writer's voice' because it approximates the 'sound' of the writer reading their piece aloud to an audience. Usually, writers convey tone through their word choice, sentence types and sentence lengths. Sometimes, punctuation marks indicate the tone. There are as many tones as there are possible attitudes and emotions.

A common way to identify a writer's tone is to read their piece aloud and then to apply an adjective(s) to define the tone. Another way is to read the piece and then ask yourself: 'Is the tone positive, negative or neutral?' Once you have decided, choose a suitable adjective to describe the tone.

The headline, 'Government environment initiative reckless', definitely conveys a negative tone by the inclusion of the word *reckless* – but what kind of negative tone? The tone could be defined more precisely with words such as *condemnatory* and *disapproving*.

Below is a list of useful words to describe tones. Ensure that you understand the meanings of these words and apply them accurately.

| Neutral tones | Positive tones | Negative tones |
|---|---|---|
| reasoned | confident | cynical |
| factual | assertive | ridiculing |
| serious | authoritative | critical |
| controlled | celebratory | disappointed |
| solemn | optimistic | pessimistic |
| sincere | approving | condemning |
| respectful | sympathetic | anxious |
| clear | nostalgic | resentful |
| calm | appreciative | dismissive |
| measured | enthusiastic | derogatory |
| formal | passionate | irritated |
| matter-of-fact | hopeful | disgusted |
| open-minded | supportive | defensive |

Expand your vocabulary to describe tone by categorising each word in the list on the next page into the most appropriate column of the table that follows. Ensure that you understand the meaning of these words and apply them accurately.

Identifying the tone of a spoken or written text is important in determining meaning.

| | | | | |
|---|---|---|---|---|
| detached | gushing | preaching | determined | fervent |
| expressive | frank | amused | spirited | insensitive |
| insulting | apologetic | bitter | cheerful | baffled |
| straightforward | understanding | astonished | mocking | grave |
| blaming | guarded | outraged | conservative | frivolous |
| businesslike | sarcastic | aggressive | scathing | pleading |
| stubborn | regretful | sensible | definite | acquiescent |
| indifferent | patriotic | condescending | confrontational | humorous |

| Neutral tones | Positive tones | Negative tones | |
|---|---|---|---|
| | | | |

**1** Below is a selection of passages and headlines from news articles responding to a range of issues of public concern. Using the vocabulary lists above, identify the tone of the writer in each case. In some cases, there may be a change in tone.

**a** 'Felled giants lie grey and burnt on the hillside, like discarded bones on funeral pyre.' (Old-growth forest logging)

______________________________

**b** 'The police need to be reminded that, at all times, they are accountable to the public, and that reaching for their guns is a last, desperate resort.' (Police shootings)

______________________________

**c** 'Decriminalise marijuana, now!' (Decriminalisation of drugs)

______________________________

**d** 'Will the government ban couples from reproducing if their embryos are found to be less than perfect?' (IVF and genetics)

______________________________

**e** 'Gambling is the scourge of this state!' (Gambling crisis)

______________________________

**f** 'An out-of-control drag race on the Princes Highway resulted in several arrests.' (Drag racing)

**g** 'Gun laws pathetic' (Gun ownership)

**h** 'Australian suburbs are being menaced by gangs of teenage gatecrashers weekend after weekend after weekend. When will parents take some responsibility?' (Teenage parties)

**i** 'Whaling is just another example of our environmental terrorism.' (Whaling)

**j** 'Footballers who misbehave in public deserve all the censure they get. They should cop it like a good sport!' (Footballer misdemeanours)

**k** 'Our public transport system is a shambles.' (Cancelled and late trains)

**l** 'Violent computer games are training our children to become the terrorists of the future.' (Impact of computer gaming)

**m** 'Without proper funding and resources, our public schools are failing our students.' (Government education funding)

**n** 'Stem-cell research offers hope in the scientific quest for a cure for cancers and other life-destroying illnesses.' (Stem-cell research)

**o** 'With all of our troops undertaking peacekeeping missions in the Middle East and the Pacific, who is looking after Australia?' (Military commitments)

**p** 'What is so recreational and relaxing about blood sports such as duck shooting and big-game fishing?' (Blood sports)

**q** 'Federal budget misses the mark' (Federal budget)

r 'An elderly man was charged with manslaughter after assisting his terminally ill wife with suicide.' (Euthanasia)

______________________________

s 'I'm eternally grateful to all of my mentors – this award represents their belief in me.' (Award speech)

______________________________

**2** Find headlines in a current newspaper that illustrate the following tones.

a Humorous: ______________________________

______________________________

b Serious: ______________________________

______________________________

c Alarmist: ______________________________

______________________________

d Celebratory: ______________________________

______________________________

e Formal: ______________________________

______________________________

f Hopeful: ______________________________

______________________________

## SPELLING FOCUS

The following words appear in this unit. Add a tick next to the ones that are spelt correctly and a cross next to the ones that are spelt incorrectly. Write the correct spelling in the space next to the words spelt incorrectly.

| | | | | | |
|---|---|---|---|---|---|
| attitude | [ ] | | optamistick | [ ] | |
| authoritative | [ ] | | dissappointed | [ ] | |
| condemming | [ ] | | confrontational | [ ] | |
| acquiesant | [ ] | | condescending | [ ] | |

| Name: | Due date: | Guardian signature: |
|---|---|---|

# 21 AUDIENCE AND PURPOSE

The grammar of reading, writing and viewing texts

The purpose of a written, spoken or visual text can be defined by an author's intentions, reasons and focus in creating that particular text. Texts may contain a **single purpose** with a narrow focus, such as the instructions for a recipe. Some texts may have **multiple purposes** with a wider focus. Although there may be a dominant purpose, a feature article on a current event may inform, persuade and entertain the reader all at once.

Some authors determine their purpose(s) according to whether they will write in a persuasive, informative, creative or instructional style. While authors may have their own personal reasons for creating a text, they may determine their purpose according to the impact they wish to have on their audience and the way they wish to present their ideas. Authors may clarify their purpose by using terms such as *to explore*, *to hypothesise*, *to advise*, *to entertain*, *to clarify*, *to propose*, *to analyse*, *to describe*, *to compare*, *to record*, *to amuse*, *to reflect*, *to promote*, *to represent*, *to explain*, *to document*, *to report*, *to define*, *to debate* and *to criticise*.

In deciding on a **target audience**, authors ask: 'Who am I writing for?' A further question could be 'How can I best engage my audience?' An author might choose a familiar audience or an unfamiliar audience. The author must have a clear target audience profile. Some aspects that need to be considered are gender, age/generation, cultural/ethnic background, socioeconomic position, political/social/spiritual/moral beliefs, interests and preoccupations, community identity and possibly common life experiences. Having a clear picture of the target audience will assist in making decisions about content, structure and language, which will best position the audience to be receptive to the text.

**1** Draw lines to match the writing styles below with the type of text that style would best suit.

| Writing style | Type of text |
|---|---|
| Informative | Letter to the editor (for publication in a newspaper) |
| Instructional | Fiction novel |
| Creative | Brochure advertising free events in the city |
| Persuasive | Directions for installing a security system |

**2** For each type of publication below, underline the purpose – to persuade, entertain or instruct.

**a** A brochure about how to manage Type 1 diabetes

persuade entertain instruct

**b** A short story about a flying pig

persuade entertain instruct

Identifying audience and purpose is the first step in reading or writing a text.

**3** Choose the best target audience from the diagram below for the texts described.

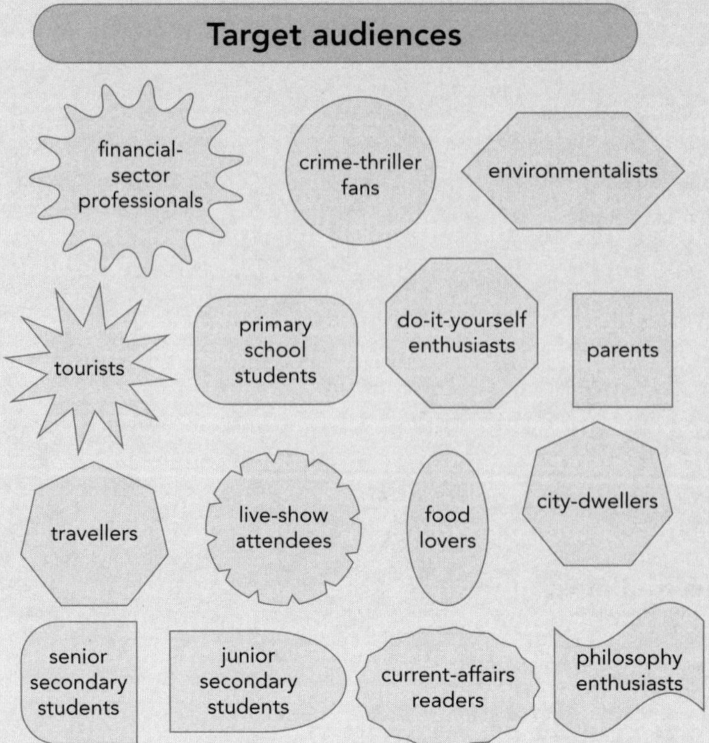


**a** A book of Italian culture and recipes with full-page colour photos

**b** The story of a young boy's quest for hidden treasure

**c** A guide on sightseeing in the Philippines

**d** An instruction manual on kitchen renovations

**e** An investigative report on political leaders

**f** A picture book illustrating the alphabet

**g** A novel about the rites of passage of a teenage girl living in a country town

**h** A report on global warming

**i** A guide to financial planning

**j** An essay about the place of religion in society

**k** A history of the Australian theatre scene

**l** A family medical guide

**m** A brochure about Neighbourhood Watch

**n** A novel about a crime within a crime

**o** A web page about things to do in Brisbane

## TAKE IT FURTHER

**1** Choose three of your current textbooks and write a one-sentence statement of purpose for each of them. You could incorporate some of the terminology used in the explanation text at the beginning of the unit.

**2** Create a target audience profile of your classmates based on the aspects outlined in the explanation text.

**3** Study a newspaper. Consider the target socioeconomic group the newspaper is aimed at. How can you tell the target socioeconomic group from the features of the newspaper?

**4** The purpose of a piece of writing may be clarified by the use of terms such as:

| | | | |
|---|---|---|---|
| to explore | to clarify | to compare | to reflect |
| to hypothesise | to propose | to persuade | to promote |
| to advise | to analyse | to record | to represent |
| to entertain | to describe | to amuse | to explain |

Read the following extracts and identify the purpose(s) of each, choosing from the list above.

**a** Our suburb is in desperate need of a community centre. However, the Council's proposal to build this amenity on local parkland is foolish. We have very few open spaces as it is! The Council should consider purchasing the recently vacated factory warehouse on David Street and remodel it as the much-needed community centre.

**b** The newly released blu-ray box set contains all of the films made by Alfred Hitchcock, including a bonus disc of Alfred Hitchcock Presents. Hitchcock fans will be enthralled with the chills and thrills of such classics as *Psycho*, *The Birds*, *Rear Window* and *Vertigo*.

**c** Carnarvon Gorge in central Queensland is a beautiful oasis that offers a spectacular holiday destination for dedicated walkers. The walking trail zigzags along the gorge and takes in striking natural formations, rare plants and aboriginal artworks.

**d** *Paper Models*: This scrapbook-style magazine includes 10 coloured paper model outlines for primary school children to create. Kids can create and learn about a farm, a medieval village, a castle, the Eiffel Tower and the pyramids. Hours of fun and education for the whole family.

## SPELLING FOCUS

The following words are part of the metalanguage of English – that is, the words we use when writing or talking about English as a subject. Make sure you can spell them all. Test yourself or work with a partner and test each other.

| | | | |
|---|---|---|---|
| advice | hypothesise | author | informative |
| clarification | persuasion | explain | clarify |
| hypothesis | audience | information | explanation |
| persuade | entertainment | purpose | intention |
| advise | inform | authorial | |
| entertain | persuasive | explanatory | |

Name: | Due date: | Guardian signature:

# 22 DIFFERENTIAL READINGS

The grammar of reading, writing and viewing texts

Not so long ago, students of English believed that there was one correct reading of every text. They also believed that their teachers knew what that true reading was, and that their task was simply to reproduce that reading in their essays. However, during the last part of the 20th century, literary critics formalised the growing idea that it was impossible to read a text in isolation or as having an absolute meaning. As you know from class discussions, everyone responds differently to a text. Any reading of a text involves the following components:

- → the author's point of view
- → the author's purpose
- → the context in which the text was created
- → the context in which the text is set
- → the experiences and knowledge the reader brings to the text
- → the reader's response to and synthesis of all of the elements listed above.

So, there are many possible and plausible readings of a text and it is now legitimate to read texts in different ways. By discussing texts with other students, you will no doubt realise that this already takes place informally.

All texts are **constructed**; that is, they are deliberately composed to get readers to respond in a certain way. This is as true of an advertisement on a billboard as it is of the plays of Shakespeare. Texts are constructed to produce a preferred or **dominant** (or invited) **reading**: interpretations that reflect dominant cultural beliefs and structures. If, for example, you are watching a film, you might become very involved in the lives of the characters – reacting almost as if they are real people. The scriptwriter and director have positioned you to respond like that: the success of the film depends on you being engaged.

There may also be **alternative readings**; that is, other interpretations that might be different but are nevertheless acceptable in cultural terms. While watching the film, for example, you might notice that the women are all exceptionally beautiful and the men are all handsome – something that is not necessarily reflected in real life. Part of your consciousness will notice that you are being positioned to accept as real a world that is not real; at the same time, you will continue to enjoy the plot twists and character revelations.

There are also **resistant readings**; that is, interpretations that challenge the accepted views within society or oppose the dominant cultural mores. Resistant readings often focus on minor characters in a text: characters who may have been silenced by the author. A resistant reading of a film might focus on the way gender roles are represented, for example, and might take the view that the representation of these roles is actually demeaning and offensive. The resistant reader is very aware of being positioned by the constructed text.

**1** Find a glossy advertisement from a magazine advertising a product that is aimed at teenagers. In a small group, analyse the advertisement.

- **a** What is the dominant or invited reading? In other words, what response is expected from the reader? How is the text constructed to ensure this response?
- **b** Are there possible alternative readings?
- **c** What would be a resistant reading to this text?

Readers read texts differently depending on the personal, social, historical and cultural context in which they read them.

**2** a Select one of your study texts and develop at least two different readings of it.
b Create a dominant reading and a resistant reading.
c Explain how each reading interprets the text and the reasons for your choice of readings.

**Some readings of texts can be grouped into categories that share certain approaches to texts. Here are some of the characteristics of different types of readings:**

- → **Gender readings** examine ideas of masculinity and femininity in texts: what those concepts mean at any given time, and how they may influence and even direct ways in which texts are both constructed and read. They are most often seen in feminist readings, in which texts are viewed from a female point of view and in the knowledge that females are often ascribed different roles, responsibilities and even different ways of thinking and acting from men.
- → **Feminist readings** deal with the oppression of women and the power relationships that contribute to that situation. They concentrate on the position of women in society and in relationships, often challenging the common assumptions made by both writers and readers of texts.
- → **Marxist readings** adopt a 'conflict model' of society headed by the ruling class, which is usually the dominant voice in literary texts. Class is the dominant feature. It is also the feature that denies or supports achievement of potential, desires, wealth, love and so on.
- → **Post-colonial readings** deal with or arise from the process of colonisation in previous centuries and national independence in (largely) the 20th century. They relate to the literature that arose from colonisation, both supporting and challenging the effects of that process. They also very often relate to issues of identity that had been suppressed or supplanted by colonial rule.
- → **Psychological readings** deal with the underlying psychology of the writer and/or the unconscious motivations of characters. They examine the ideas that underpin and support the social fabric: the cultural/social identity on which personal identity is built. They include the narrower psychoanalytic readings which, while based on the same material, use and interpret writers, characters and texts in terms of specific symbols; for example, Freudian symbols and terminology.

**1** A famous reading of *Hamlet* explained Hamlet's character totally in terms of his relationship with his mother and his sexual jealousy of his new stepfather.

What kind of reading was this: a feminist reading, a Marxist reading, a post-colonial reading or a psychological reading?

**2** Another reading of Hamlet concentrated on the character of Ophelia and attributed her madness to the fact that the men in her life refused to listen to her.

What kind of reading was this: a feminist reading, a Marxist reading, a post-colonial reading or a Freudian reading?

**3** In the 1970s, the critic Arnold Kettle wrote an interpretation of Emily Brontë's powerful story of destructive passion, *Wuthering Heights*, in which he saw the causes of the tragedy in the very different social positions of the lovers. Cathy, as the daughter of the owner of the Heights, would have been humiliated to marry Heathcliff, who has no social position or property. He takes revenge for his rejection by acquiring such social status and property that he can be master over his rival's family.

What kind of reading was this: a feminist reading, a Marxist reading, a post-colonial reading or a Freudian reading?

**4** A film version of Jane Austen's *Mansfield Park* shocked viewers when it made the point that the wealth of the main family in the story would have been based on the profits of the slave trade.

What kind of reading was this: a feminist reading, a Marxist reading, a post-colonial reading or a Freudian reading?

**5** A critic writing about Roald Dahl's famous autobiography of his childhood, *Boy*, made the point that Dahl is an elitist who always treats servants and social inferiors with contempt and rudeness.

What kind of reading was this: a feminist reading, a Marxist reading, a post-colonial reading or a Freudian reading?

**6** A South Korean director staged a version of Shakespeare's *Macbeth* in which Lady Macbeth became the main character. The play was even called *Lady Macbeth*.

What kind of reading was this: a feminist reading, a Marxist reading, a post-colonial reading or a Freudian reading?

**7** Here are some readings of Charlotte Brontë's novel *Jane Eyre*.

→ Reading 1: *Jane Eyre* is one of the greatest love stories of all time. Jane and Rochester are twin souls and their love survives and triumphs over the most terrible obstacles. Like all great romances, the novel ends with the lovers united.

→ Reading 2: *Jane Eyre* is above all a Gothic novel, with all the elements of the genre: a mad woman in the attic, screams in the night, the horror of the fire, the Gothic mansion, a Byronic hero. It was written at a time when this genre was at its peak of popularity, and would have been read by Brontë's contemporaries as an example of the genre.

→ Reading 3: *Jane Eyre* is about class. Although well educated, Jane, as a governess, is part of the servant class. She is humiliated by visitors to Thornhill and she is powerless because of her social status.

→ Reading 4: *Jane Eyre* is about the patriarchal Victorian society. Jane struggles to assert her independence and self-worth as a woman and refuses to accept the roles that society has decreed for her.

→ Reading 5: In *Jane Eyre*, Rochester's wealth is built on exploitation of the people of the Caribbean. This aspect of the novel was highlighted in another novel, *The Wide Sargasso Sea*, which tells the story from the point of view of Rochester's Caribbean wife, the woman who became the mad woman in the attic.

**a** Which of these readings takes a Marxist approach? __________

**b** Which of these readings takes a post-colonial approach? __________

**c** Which of these readings takes a feminist approach? __________

**d** Two of these readings focus on the genre of the book. Which readings are they?

__________

**8** Write a paragraph about the things you have learnt from this brief look at different readings of texts. Include a comment on how the techniques have helped you to progress to a more complex interaction with the texts, and give specific examples.

## SPELLING FOCUS

The words below are associated with the work that you have done in this unit. Many of them are part of the metalanguage of English. Make sure you can spell them all. Test yourself or work with a partner and test each other.

| | | | |
|---|---|---|---|
| alternative | psychological | resistant | interpretation |
| Freudian | dominant | post-colonial | gender |
| Marxist | genre | feminist | reading |

Name: | Due date: | Guardian signature:

# 23 THE NOVEL

The grammar of reading, writing and viewing texts

A **novel** is an extended work of prose fiction, a narrative, a 'fictitious prose narrative of considerable length' (*Macquarie Dictionary*, Macquarie Dictionary Publishers 2016). It allows the writer (and the reader) the opportunity to explore complex and detailed plots, themes, characters and settings. There are two major features that provide a useful starting point for novel analysis: novels tell a story, and they examine the tensions between individuals and the societies in which they live.

Our engagement as readers begins here and progresses to a more sophisticated appreciation of the variety and intricacies of characters and of their societies. In this way we can examine both the plot or subject (concerned with the story and the characters) and the discourse of a novel (concerned with the themes and texture of the writing). **Plot** is concerned with *what* happens. **Discourse** is concerned with *how* and *why* it happens. These aspects are also related to audience, context and purpose (see Unit 21). Elements of discourse include the following.

1. **Narrative point of view:** the decisions an author makes about *how* the story will be conveyed
   - → Is it narrated in the first (*I*) or third person (*she/he*)?
   - → Is the narrator omniscient (all-knowing) or limited?
   - → Is the narrator a participant in the action of the novel?
   - → Is the narrator (or perhaps the author) intrusive? If so, where and in what way? What is the effect?
   - → Can the narrator be trusted?
2. **Structure:** the mechanics of the novel's presentation
   - → Is the novel presented in chapters or parts/sections?
   - → Is the novel presented by means of letters, conversations, diary entries, memories/reflections?
   - → Is there more than one narrator? How is each one used? Are they telling the same story or different parts of it?
3. **Style:** the author's patterns of language use. This feature – common to all writers – represents an individual voice reflecting much about the author's unique situation and development, as well as the conscious choices the author has made about language in the context of the novel and its setting.
   - → Is the vocabulary historical, contemporary, formal, vernacular (and so on)?
   - → What sorts of imagery does the writer use? Are particular words, phrases or images repeated?
   - → Are images or symbols associated with specific characters or situations?
   - → Are there features within the text that operate as symbols?
4. **Characters:** the discourse is also to be found in individuals or groups of characters
   - → Who are the major characters?
   - → What does a detailed character study tell you about them – about their function in the text? (For extra information about character analysis, refer to Unit 24).
5. **Themes** are the driving force behind the discourse. We discover what the author really wanted to say in constructing the work and we are able to explore those motivating ideas
   - → What are the main ideas discussed in the text?
   - → What are the views of individual characters about those ideas?
   - → What do characters, situations and settings convey to the reader about the themes?

These explanations and questions are designed to highlight and explore the 'constructedness' of texts. Novels contain entire worlds within their pages and those worlds are constructed realities; that is, what we find there is meant to be there and therefore forms the legitimate basis for further investigation and critical exploration.

A knowledge of the metalanguage (terms such as 'plot' and 'setting') is essential to the study of the novel.

Read the extract below, from *Heart of Darkness* by Joseph Conrad.

The sea-reach of the Thames stretched before us like the beginning of an interminable waterway. In the offing the sea and the sky were welded together without a joint, and in the luminous space the tanned sails of the barges drifting up with the tide seemed to stand still in red clusters of canvas sharply peaked, with gleams of varnished sprits. A haze rested on the low shores that ran out to sea in vanishing flatness. The air was dark above Gravesend, and farther back still seemed condensed into a mournful gloom, brooding motionless over the biggest, and the greatest, town on earth … Marlow sat cross-legged right aft, leaning against the mizzen-mast. He had sunken cheeks, a yellow complexion, a straight back, an ascetic aspect, and, with his arms dropped, the palms of hands outwards, resembled an idol.

We exchanged a few words lazily. Afterwards there was silence on board the yacht … We felt meditative, and fit for nothing … The day was ending in a serenity of still and exquisite brilliance. The water shone pacifically; the sky, without a speck, was a benign immensity of unstained light … Only the gloom to the west, brooding over the upper reaches, became more sombre every minute, as if angered by the approach of the sun.

Forthwith a change came over the waters, and the serenity became less brilliant but more profound. The old river in its broad reach rested unruffled at the decline of day, after ages of good service done to the race that peopled its banks, spread out in the tranquil dignity of a waterway leading to the uttermost ends of the earth. What greatness had not floated on the ebb of that river into the mystery of an unknown earth! …

And farther west on the upper reaches the place of the monstrous town was still marked ominously on the sky, a brooding gloom in sunshine, a lurid glare under the stars. 'And this also,' said Marlow suddenly, 'has been one of the dark places of the earth.'

'Now when I was a little chap I had a passion for maps. I would look for hours at South America, or Africa, or Australia, and lose myself in all the glories of exploration. At that time there were many blank spaces on the earth, and when I saw one that looked particularly inviting on a map (but they all look that) I would put my finger on it and say, 'When I grow up I will go there.' The North Pole was one of these places, I remember. Well, I haven't been there yet, and shall not try now. The glamour's off. Other places were scattered about the Equator, and in every sort of latitude all over the two hemispheres. I have been in some of them, and … well, we won't talk about that. But there was one yet – the biggest, the most blank, so to speak – that I had a hankering after …' He was silent for a while.

'… No, it is impossible; it is impossible to convey the life-sensation of any given epoch of one's existence – that which makes its truth, its meaning – its subtle and penetrating essence. It is impossible. We live, as we dream – alone …' He paused again as if reflecting, then added, 'Of course in this you fellows see more than I could then. You see me, whom you know …'

It had become so pitch dark that we listeners could hardly see one another. For a long time already he, sitting apart, had been no more to us than a voice. There was not a word from anybody. The others might have been asleep, but I was awake. I listened, I listened on the watch for the sentence, for the word, that would give me the [clue] to the faint uneasiness inspired by this narrative that seemed to shape itself without human lips in the heavy night-air of the river.

Conrad, J 1899, *The Heart of Darkness*, OUP World Classic Edition, 1990, pp. 133–4.

**1** a What is the narrative point of view in the extract?

b Whose voice do we hear?

**2** The extract is written using first-person narration but, unusually, the plural pronoun is used at first and then 'we' changes to 'I'. What is the effect of the use of the first-person plural pronoun?

**3** a One character is emerging as the protagonist (main character). Who is it?

b What impression is being created of that character in this extract?

**4** How important is the use of dialogue in establishing the character? Explain your answer.

**5** Is the author building up a sense of mystery about Marlow? If so, how?

**6** The extract begins with a detailed description of the setting. What is the mood that is established by this description? Which words or phrases are most effective in establishing this mood?

**7** The authenticity of a description can be enhanced by the use of specialist or technical vocabulary. What technical words does Conrad use to describe the vessels on the Thames?

**8** How is a sense of isolation created in the last paragraph of the extract?

**9** Does the author succeed in creating suspense? Explain your answer.

One of the most popular genres is the **quest narrative**, also called 'the hero's journey'. This genre has specific features and narrative development. Here is a summary.

- → Ordinary world – the hero is introduced in their usual environment.
- → Call to adventure – the hero faces a problem, conflict, challenge or goal.
- → Refusal of the call – the hero is reluctant to take on the call to adventure.
- → Mentor – a wise person (or creature) enters the hero's life and gives encouraging advice (this may also include training, magical equipment and so on).
- → The first threshold – the hero makes the decision to take on the call to adventure and leaves their 'ordinary world' for the quest in the 'special world'.
- → Tests, allies, enemies – the hero begins to learn about the 'special world' and the demands of the quest and responds with newly developed talents and skills.
- → Approaching the innermost cave – the hero reaches a 'dangerous place' close to the goal.
- → The supreme ordeal – the hero is confronted with further problems and obstacles after entering the 'innermost cave' and encounters a real (or symbolic) life-or-death moment, which causes some change in the hero's character.
- → Reward – the hero achieves the goal.
- → The road back – the hero begins the return journey to the 'ordinary world' and encounters some obstacles and dangers in doing so.
- → Resurrection – the hero is tested for a final time and gains new insights.
- → Return with the elixir – the hero arrives home with the 'treasure' or 'lessons' that have been gained while in the 'special world'.

**1** Discuss the features of a hero journey/quest narrative with which you are familiar. Summarise these features in your workbook.

**2** Using the narrative quest outlined in the explanation box above, write your own synopsis (outline) for a quest narrative novel in your workbook.

The words below are associated with the work that you have done in this unit. Make sure you can spell them all. Test yourself or work with a partner and test each other.

| | | | |
|---|---|---|---|
| character | omniscient | contemporary | participator |
| discourse | structure | historical | symbol |
| narrative | symbolic | narrator | vernacular |

Name: | Due date: | Guardian signature:

# 24 THE SHORT STORY

The grammar of reading, writing and viewing texts

The **short story** ('any brief piece of fictional prose') is a popular text form. It does not have a prescribed length or a prescribed structure. Short stories of various kinds have been in existence for thousands of years. Myths, legends, fables and parables are all ancestors of the short story, as are traditional tales such as the German *Märchen*, the Russian *Skaz* and the Chinese *Ping Hua*. Such a hybrid ancestry is no doubt part of the reason for the short story's complexity.

Prior to the mid-20th century it was considered important for the short story to demonstrate symmetry of plot: it should have a beginning, a middle and an end – often a 'surprise' end. In some contemporary short stories, however, there do not appear to be any 'proper' endings, perhaps reflecting real life, which often lacks structure and shape.

The beginning–middle–end structure (or lack of it) actually gives the reader valuable information about the cultural context and expectations of the writer's society.

The main questions to ask about the plot are: 'What is included?' and 'What is omitted, and why?' The short story is a totally constructed 'reality' and conscious decisions have been made about what will or will not be included.

**Indirect characterisation** is a process of revelation based on such elements as a character's physical appearance, response to the environment, values as expressed in their comments and actions, and the way they fit into the wider context of society.

**Direct characterisation** occurs where the reader is directly told things about a character, usually by a narrator.

**Narrative structure** is an important element in any piece of fiction. You should be asking yourself the following questions: 'What do you know?', 'How do you know it?', 'From where do you get your information?' and 'Is the narration in the first, second or third person?' (See Unit 23 p. 63.)

Both physical and emotional settings are central elements of any short story. Asking where the action takes place and when it takes place will reveal the social and cultural context of the narrator and of the story.

The themes of any work exist because the author wants to say something about a particular topic. It is important not to confuse the theme(s) with the **subject** of the story. For example, a writer may wish to explore the nature of father–son relationships (the theme) and will do so by writing a story about a driving lesson involving a father and son (the subject).

Read the extract of the short story below by Henry Lawson and complete the exercises that follow.

'I'd been away from home for eight years,' said Mitchell to his mate, as they dropped their swags in the mulga shade and sat down. 'I hadn't written a letter – kept putting it off, and a blundering fool of a fellow that got down the day before me told the old folks that he'd heard I was dead.' Here he took a pull at his waterbag.

'When I got home they were all in mourning for me. It was night, and the girl that opened the door screamed and fainted away like a shot.' He lit his pipe.

**Modern short stories do not always follow the traditional pattern of narrative.**

'Mother was upstairs howling and moaning in a chair, with all the girls boohooing round her for company. The old man was sitting in the back kitchen crying to himself.' He put his hat down on the ground, dinted in the crown, and poured some water into the hollow for his cattle-pup.

'The girls came rushing down. Mother was so pumped out that she couldn't get up. They thought at first I was a ghost, and then they all tried to get hold of me at once – nearly smothered me. Look at that pup! You want to carry a tank of water on a dry stretch when you've got a pup that drinks as much as two men.' He poured a drop more water into the top of his hat.

'Well, mother screamed and nearly fainted when she saw me. Such a picnic you never saw. They kept it up all night. I thought the old cove was gone off his chump. The old woman wouldn't let go of my hand for three mortal hours. Have you got the knife?'

He cut up some more tobacco.

'All next day the house was full of neighbours, and the first to come was an old sweetheart of mine. I never thought that she cared for me till then. Mother and the girls made me swear never to go away any more; and they kept watching me, and hardly let me go outside for fear I'd—'

'Get drunk?'

'No – you're smart – for fear I'd clear. At last I swore on the Bible that I'd never leave home while the old folks were alive; and then mother seemed easier in her mind.'

He rolled the pup over and examined its feet. 'I expect I'll have to carry him a bit – his feet are very sore. Well, he's done pretty well this morning, and anyway he won't drink so much when he's carried.'

'You broke your promise about leaving home,' said his mate. Mitchell stood up, stretched himself, and looked dolefully from his heavy swag to the wide, hot, shadeless cotton-bush plain ahead.

'Oh, yes,' he yawned, 'I stopped at home for a week, and then they began to growl because I couldn't get any work to do.'

The mate guffawed and Mitchell grinned. They shouldered the swags, with the pup on top of Mitchell's, took up their billies and waterbags, turned their unshaven faces to the wide, hazy distance, and left the timber behind them.

Lawson, H 1893, 'On the edge of a plain', *The Penguin Henry Lawson Short Stories*, ed. Barnes, 1986.

**1** **a** Summarise the plot in no more than 50 words.

**b** What is the form of the text? Would the text work in any other form? Which form? Why?

**c** Find examples of details that are used to recreate time and place.

d What is the cultural setting (look at elements of gender, class, geography)?

e Is the language used appropriate to the genre and setting?

f What is the narrative structure of the short story? Who is the narrator? Does this influence the way the story is told?

g What are the major themes? How do the characters' words or actions help establish and develop these themes?

**2** a How are the roles of men and women depicted by Mitchell?

b What does his attitude tell the reader about the gender expectations of the characters?

c What does the story tell us about his attitude to women?

d Are these expectations and attitudes different from those of today?

## TAKE IT FURTHER

**1** Make a plan for an original short narrative by completing the following questions.

a What is the setting – place/location (interior/exterior)?

b What is the setting – time period (day/hour/era/season)?

c Who is the main character (protagonist) – name/age/appearance?

**d** What is the protagonist like (general description of personality)?

**e** In the narrative, does the protagonist have a problem/conflict/goal? What is it?

**f** Why is it so important for the protagonist to achieve the goal or solve the problem?

**g** What is the source of the conflict/problem in the narrative?

**h** Who/What is the antagonist in the narrative?

**i** Why is it so important to the antagonist to oppose the protagonist in this narrative?

**j** Which additional characters might contribute to the narrative?

**k** How and when does the narrative start?

**l** How and when does the narrative finish?

**m** What is the time frame of the narrative?

**n** What are the main dramatic scenes or moments in this narrative?

**o** What is the viewpoint in the narrative – that is, who tells the events?

**2** Use your plan to write the short narrative in your workbook or on a computer/laptop. Assess whether it was necessary to deviate from your plan during writing, and why.

**SPELLING FOCUS**

The words below are associated with the work that you have done in this unit. Make sure you can spell them all. Test yourself or work with a partner and test each other.

| | | | |
|---|---|---|---|
| antagonist | historical | appearance | viewpoint |
| contemporary | narrator | dramatic | protagonist |
| antagonist | scene | goal | |

Name: | Due date: | Guardian signature:

# 25 THE POEM

The grammar of reading, writing and viewing texts

| Form | Structural features | Language features | Examples |
|---|---|---|---|
| Ballad | Narrative poem<br>Quatrain: four-line verse<br>Question/answer format<br>Dialogue format | Repetition of lines, words, phrases (refrain)<br>End rhyme scheme: AABB or ABAB<br>Regular rhythm, suitable to be set to music, as was tradition for ballads<br>Common use of dialect words reflecting the speech of the time and place | 'Lord Randal' (Anonymous)<br>'The wreck of the Hesperus' (Henry W Longfellow)<br>'Clancy of the overflow' (Banjo Paterson) |
| Sonnet | Love and metaphysical themes<br>Classic sonnets have 14 lines: an octave (stanza of 8 lines) plus a sestet (stanza of 6 lines)<br>OR<br>Shakespearian sonnets have three quatrains of four lines and a concluding couplet | Classic sonnet end rhyme scheme: ABBA, ABBA, CDECDE<br>Shakespearean sonnet end rhyme scheme: ABABCDCDEFEFGG<br>Figurative language: symbols, metaphors, similes<br>Alliteration<br>Assonance<br>Rhythm: iambic pentameter | 'Shall I compare thee to a summer's day'? (Shakespeare)<br>'Suburban sonnet' (Gwen Harwood)<br>'Batter my heart' (John Donne) |

**1** John O'Brien's comic ballad 'Said Hanrahan' draws on the traditional ballad form.

'We'll all be rooned,' said Hanrahan,
In accents most forlorn,
Outside the church, ere Mass began,
One frosty Sunday morn.

O'Brien, J (Patrick Joseph Hartigan) 1921, 'Said Hanrahan', stanza 1.

**a** What is the the rhyme scheme? How does it contribute to the comic effect?

**b** Is the rhythm regular?

The titles of poems are in quote marks, not italics.

**c** How has the poet used dialogue to reflect the time and place?

**2** In 'Sonnet 130' Shakespeare uses the form of the sonnet (as a love poem) to undercut the nature of the poet's romantic relationship with his goddess-like love. Read the sonnet.

## Sonnet 130

My mistress' eyes are nothing like the sun;
Coral is far more red than her lips' red:
If snow be white, why then her breasts are dun;
If hairs be wires, black wires grow on her head.
I have seen roses damask'd, red and white,
But no such roses see I in her cheeks;
And in some perfumes is there more delight
Than in the breath that from my mistress reeks.
I love to hear her speak, yet well I know
That music hath a far more pleasing sound.
I grant I never saw a goddess go:
My mistress, when she walks, treads on the ground.
And yet, by heaven, I think my love as rare
As any she belied with false compare.

Shakespeare, W 1609, 'Sonnet 130'

**a** Explain how the poet describes the object of his affection.

**b** How does his description of her differ from what you might have expected?

**c** What is the poet actually saying about his love?

Many poets choose to write in conventional poetic forms, such as the ballad and the sonnet.

**d** Why might the poet's mistress be even more flattered by this seemingly uncomplimentary poem?

**e** In the third quatrain the poet suggests his mistress is ordinary – not something a woman would want to hear. How does the concluding couplet completely turn this around?

John Donne, a contemporary of Shakespeare's used the accepted form for love poetry to express his devotion to God. He also used contemporary mapping and images to demonstrate his commitment to God. The sonnets he wrote are dramatic and include many of the language features mentioned above. 'Holy Sonnet VII' is Donne's vision of Judgement Day, for everyone and for himself specifically.

## Holy Sonnet VII

At the round earth's imagined corners blow
Your trumpets, angels, and arise, arise
From death, you numberless infinities
Of souls, and to your scattered bodies go,
All whom the flood did, and fire shall, overthrow,
All whom war, dea[r]th, age, agues, tyrannies,
Despair, law, chance, hath slain, and you whose eyes
Shall behold God, and never taste death's woe.
But let them sleep, Lord, and me mourn a space,
For, if above all these, my sins abound,
Tis late to ask abundance of Thy grace,
When we are there. Here on this lowly ground,
Teach me how to repent; for that's as good
As if Thou hadst sealed my pardon, with Thy blood.

Donne, J 1633, 'Holy Sonnet VII'

**1** In 'Holy Sonnet VII' find examples of the following language features.

**a** Figurative language: alliteration and assonance

Alliteration:

Assonance:

**b** Rhythm: iambic pentameter

**2** **a** What is the rhyme scheme?

**b** This rhyme scheme is different from that of either the classic sonnet or the typical Shakespearean sonnet. What is the effect of using the same two rhymes of the octave (the first eight lines)?

**3** There is a tension in the image in line 1 between the 'round earth' and its 'imagined corners'. Which wider (philosophical) tension do these two aspects reflect?

**4** Where is the volta (turning point in theme, image or tone)?

**5** What is the mood of the octave?

**6** In what way does this mood alter in the sestet (the last six lines)?

**SPELLING FOCUS**

The words below are associated with the work that you have done in this unit. Make sure you can spell them all. Test yourself or work with a partner and test each other.

| | | | | |
|---|---|---|---|---|
| couplet | rhyme | octave | syllable | rhythm |
| narrative | structural | poetry | iambic | stanza |
| poet | dialogue | sestet | pentameter | volta |

Name: | Due date: | Guardian signature:

# 26 THE PLAY

The grammar of reading, writing and viewing texts

Traditional **plays** have a one, two or three (or sometimes five) act structure. Act One contains an **exposition** in which the 'who', 'what', 'where' and 'when' are established. The exposition section also contains several fundamental aspects to begin a series of dramatic actions. Most plays begin at the '**point of attack**' – just before the central conflict occurs – through an **inciting incident** that introduces the conflict. Many playwrights instigate the inciting incident through explosive statements or dialogue, a physical action or a stage direction involving theatrical production elements. This incident raises a **dramatic question** (or chain of dramatic questions), which will engage the viewer through curiosity or suspense. Act Two shows how the central conflict builds up through **complications** and **turning points** towards a **resolution**. Finally, Act Three rises towards the resolution of the central conflict and answers the dramatic question(s) – decisions are undertaken, mysteries are explained and the defeated make an exit.

As drama is communicated through the speeches, behaviours and actions of dramatic persons, **characters** are essential in a play. The most credible characters are recognisable types with some unique or complex personal qualities. Audiences gain insights into characters through the following: stage directions; what they say; what they do; what other characters say about a particular character; and how characters interact with each other.

**Dialogue** is also a tool for characterisation and plot development. The playwright may suggest how characters might speak by providing bracketed adverbs before and during a character's speech. Plays provide the playwright with the challenge of portraying real speech. Real speech is characterised by sentence fragments and a variety of sentence types, which combine to create varied sentence patterns. Often, repeated phrases and verbal ticks are evident. Contractions and superlatives shape emphasis and rhythm. Generally, real speech is informal and incorporates cultural idioms, slang, colloquialisms, clichés and buzzwords. The ethnicity of a character may be suggested through altered grammatical patterns and verbal meter. Playwrights can shape the individuality of their characters through the speech style they attribute to them, whether formal or informal.

In a play, dialogue imparts and reveals information, and directs audience attention to the plot. Dialogue is the key to establishing the tone, mood, pace and rhythm of the performance itself.

Playwrights may incorporate theatrical production elements into their scripts. These may include directions on groupings, levels, costuming, lighting, sound effects, and so on, in order to underline a dramatic point in the play.

**1** Much of the success of Arthur Miller's play *The Crucible* depends on the writer's ability to convince his audience that the characters are members of the Salem community of 1692. Consider the extract on the next page.

A play is designed to be performed, not just read.

MRS PUTNAM: This is no silly season, Rebecca. My Ruth is bewildered, Rebecca; she cannot eat.

REBECCA: Perhaps she is not hungered yet. [*To PARRIS*] I hope you are not decided to go in search of loose spirits, Mr Parris. I've heard promise of that outside.

PARRIS: A wide opinion's running in the parish that the Devil may be among us, and I would satisfy them that they are wrong.

PROCTOR: Then let you come out and call them wrong. Did you consult the wardens before you called this minister to look for devils?

PARRIS: He is not coming to look for devils!

PROCTOR: Then what's he coming for?

PUTNAM: There be children dyin' in the village, Mister!

PROCTOR: I seen none dyin'. This society will not be a bag to swing round your head, Mr Putnam. [*To PARRIS*] Did you call a meeting before you–

PUTNAM: I am sick of meetings; cannot the man turn his head without he have a meeting?

Miller, A 1953, *The Crucible*, Act One.

**a** Underline the words that are used in a different way from the way we use them today.

**b** What are the effects of these changes?

**c** Replace the words you underlined in part **a** with more contemporary ones. Read the two versions with a partner and comment on the differences.

**d** What information is imparted about the characters and the situation?

**2** Robert Bolt's play *A Man for All Seasons* follows the latter stages of the career of Henry VIII's Chancellor, Sir Thomas More. The historical narration is delivered by the character of the Common Man (who plays the roles of several lower-class characters). His speech and actions remind the audience that they are watching a play – that this is just a representation of life.

In the following extract the stage directions are very detailed.

COMMON MAN (AS THE STEWARD) [*to audience, thoughtfully*]: The great thing's not to get out of your depth … What I can tell them's common knowledge! But now they've given money for it and everyone wants value for his money. They'll make a secret of it not to prove they've not been bilked … They'll make it a secret by making it dangerous … Mm … Oh, when I can't touch the bottom I'll go deaf blind and dumb. [*Holds out coins.*] And that's more than I *earn* in a fortnight!

[*On this; a fanfare of trumpets; plainsong; the rear of the stage becomes a source of glittering blue light; Hampton Court is hoisted out of sight, and other screens are lowered one after the other, each masking the rest, bearing respectively sunflowers, hollyhocks, roses, magnolias. When the fanfare ceases the plainsong goes on quietly, and the screens throw long shadows like the shadows of trees.*]

Bolt, R 1954, *A Man for All Seasons.*

**a** What is the Common Man saying here?

**b** What is the implied advice for the audience?

**c** What sort of atmosphere do the stage directions aim to create?

**d** What elements does the playwright employ to create these?

**e** What do these elements reveal about Bolt's purpose overall?

## TAKE IT FURTHER

**1** Plan a play about two or three characters who are confronted with a dilemma. Complete the following tasks in order to develop your play. Draw on the explanation text at the beginning of this unit to assist you with structural and language features.

**a** Write a list of the characters: give names, physical descriptions (including costume) and a brief outline of their personality.

**b** Outline the exposition (who, where, when, what).

**c** Outline an inciting incident.

**d** Outline a dramatic question.

**e** Outline a complication.

**f** Outline a turning point(s).

**g** Devise the resolution.

**2** Write the opening scene of the play in your workbook. Give a description of the setting, including time of day and year. Aim to develop distinct 'voices' for your characters and indicate how they will deliver their lines in brackets after their name. You may wish to include instructions about gestures and movements. Additionally, you may draw on theatrical elements such as lighting.

**3** Use your plan to write the rest of the play in your workbook or computer/laptop. Assess whether it was necessary to deviate from your plan during writing, and why.

## SPELLING FOCUS

The words below are associated with the work that you have done in this unit. Make sure you can spell them all. Test yourself or work with a partner and test each other.

| | | | | |
|---|---|---|---|---|
| behaviour | exposition | credible | theatrical | dramatic |
| conflict | suspense | dilemma | characterisation | resolution |
| dialogue | atmosphere | playwright | curiosity | unique |

| Name: | Due date: | Guardian signature: |
|---|---|---|

# 27 THE FILM

The grammar of reading, writing and viewing texts

**Films** are narratives constructed through dialogue and images (sound and sight). Mainstream commercial films are organised in a three-act structure – **the set-up** (Act One), the **development** (Act Two) and the **resolution** (Act Three), with turning points bridging the dramatic action from act to act.

The set-up fulfils the same content demands as an **exposition** in a play (see Unit 26) and establishes the genre. There may be some **backstory** – details about the characters and situation that occurred prior to the moment that the film takes up the story. Some films use a **narrative voice over** to fill in the backstory. Many set-ups open with a central **visual image** and/or **signature sound/music**, which create a strong sense of place, mood, character or theme. This often becomes a recurring **visual motif** throughout the film, with multiple thematic implications. The **inciting incident** occurs after the set-up. In mainstream films this occurs at approximately 20 minutes into the narrative. In film terminology, this is referred to as a **catalyst** and begins the action of the story, as well as raising the dramatic question (see Unit 26).

The narrative proceeds through **beats** and **scenes**. A beat is a single dramatic moment; a series of beats build a scene. Scenes have a beginning, middle and end. They advance the story, reveal characters, explore the theme and carry visual images.

**Turning points** between acts keep the pace of the action moving. They can change the direction of the action, present a crucial moment of choice for the central character(s), highlight the dramatic question and increase the tension about solving it.

**Point of view** in a film is crucial to the viewing position from which the audience will actually 'see' the story. Like other texts, a film may be told through the point of view of one character, several characters or the omniscient point of view of the screenwriter. Generally, film scripts do not contain technical information about camera shots and angles or lighting – this is the creative task of the director who brings the script to life. Screenplays have a specific format (see 'Take it further' on page 81).

**1** Using a film or films that you know or have studied, complete the following exercises. (Note: The examples you use do not have to be taken from the same film. Write your responses in a your workbook if you do not have enough space on these pages.)

**a** Name a film that uses a backstory in the opening scenes. How is the backstory told? Is it an effective method of telling the audience what it needs to know?

**b** Name a film that begins with a dominant image. What is the image and why is it used?

Films are multimodal texts, using image, sound and language.

**c** Give an example of a scene from a film that is the inciting incident or catalyst that begins the action of the story. How has the filmmaker constructed this vital incident?

**d** Give an example of a beat in a film and comment on its place in the build-up to the scene. Why have you chosen this scene?

**e** Name a film that shows the point of view of only one character and comment on the possible reason for the filmmaker's choice.

**f** Name a film that is told from multiple points of view. From whose point of view is it told?

**g** Give an example of a film that is told from the omniscient viewpoint of the screenwriter. How effective is this technique and why has it been chosen?

**h** Name a film that makes considerable use of narrative voice over. Why is this technique used? Who is the voice? What part in the action does its character play and how might that role affect his/her narrative?

**i** Based on the explanation and questions in this unit, compile a table that will assist you in analysing a film. When you have completed the table, test it on a film you know or have studied.

The format of a screenplay is very specific. The scene heading layout includes:
→ the scene number
→ whether it is an interior or exterior location – INT/EXT (capitalised)
→ the specific location, e.g. THE LIBRARY (capitalised)
→ the time of day the scene occurs, e.g. NIGHT (capitalised).

The scene description consists of concise, concrete descriptions of the action that can be represented on screen.

Dialogue is set out with all character names in capitals; stage directions are written under the characters' names, followed by dialogue.

**1** Read the following extract from a student adaptation of Penelope Rose's short story 'First Dance'.

SC.8 INT. CHRISSY'S BEDROOM EVENING

Chrissy's bedroom is cluttered with the mess of teenagehood; radio playing. CHRISSY and TONI enter with a large bottle of Coke and glasses. TONI pours the drink. CHRISSY rummages in the back of her wardrobe. She produces a bottle of Vodka and waves it at TONI.

CHRISSY

Want some of this?

TONI

Yep, why not!

CHRISSY pours a generous serve of vodka into each Coke. The girls toast and drink.

**a** What is the scene number? ______________

**b** What is the specific location? ______________________________________

**c** What time of day is it? ______________________________________

**d** What sound effects will be required? ______________________________________

**e** What props will be required?

______________________________________________________________________________

**f** What are the basic requirements of the set?

______________________________________________________________________________

**2** Write your own screenplay adaptation of a short story or a poem or song lyric. Begin by making a list of the key characters, scenes and main dialogue below. Ensure that you include only what can be represented on screen. Set out your adaptation in correct screenplay format in your workbook.

**3** Make a plan for a feature film by completing a synopsis for each of the following narrative stages. Remember to indicate the catalyst (inciting moment), turning points and so on.

**a** Act One (the set-up):

**b** Act Two (the development):

**c** Act Three (the resolution):

**SPELLING FOCUS**

The words below are associated with the work that you have done in this unit. Many of them are part of the metalanguage of English. Make sure you can spell them all. Test yourself or work with a partner and test each other.

| catalyst | technical | terminology | voice over |
|---|---|---|---|
| inciting | tension | resolution | |

| Name: | Due date: | Guardian signature: |
|---|---|---|

# 28 VISUAL TEXTS: CARTOONS AND ADVERTISEMENTS

The grammar of reading, writing and viewing texts

**Cartoons** are personal creative responses that usually combine images and text to make a serious point through the use of humour. They interpret or comment on matters of public interest by presenting a single message. Cartoonists employ a range of visual and verbal strategies to convey their ideas:

- → **Caricatures:** the exaggeration of physical features to illustrate an idea. Public figures are often the target of caricature.
- → **Anthropomorphism:** the representation of animals or other non-human entities with human features to comment on human behaviour; for example, a snarling dog or snorting pig with the facial features of a politician.
- → **Symbols:** recognisable objects and signs that convey an idea; for example, a dove with an olive branch generally represents peace.
- → **Visual association:** suggested links and comparisons between two objects, scenes or people. Disreputable people have been represented as Adolf Hitler; powerful female politicians have been represented as Lara Croft or Wonder Woman.
- → **Metaphorical references:** the use of visual and verbal metaphors to suggest that one thing is another; for example, planet Earth is often represented as a ship.
- → **Stereotypes/Homogenous groups:** representation of typical features of a type of person or group of people. For example, trade unionists may be pictured as obese 'thugs' in shorts and singlets with aggressive expressions and gestures.
- → **Punchline/Caption:** the verbal 'joke' of the cartoon; may include a range of persuasive language devices.
- → **Black humour:** a joke about a taboo topic intended to provoke serious ideas.
- → **Tone:** cartoons usually convey a single tone. Irony, sarcasm, suspicion and ridicule are common tones.

**1** Carefully examine these cartoons by Judy Horacek created for World Environment Day, June 2016.

Judy Horacek

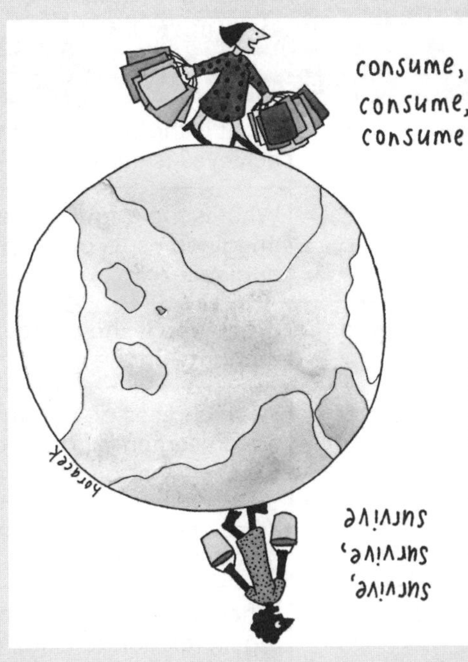


Judy Horacek

**Advertising texts use a variety of techniques to persuade readers.**

**a** Complete this paragraph framework on the 'earth-as-eaten-apple' cartoon by writing it up in your workbook. Make adjustments to sentences as appropriate.

The (image / cartoon / visual) by (artist) presents a (positive / negative/ critical / approving / disapproving) view on (state the topic / issue). The (image / cartoon / visual) depicts (brief description of image). A central symbol is (describe central symbol) which conveys the idea (explain the idea). Another notable visual feature is (describe notable visual feature) which represents the idea (explain the idea). The (image / cartoon / visual) contains a metaphorical reference to (identify metaphorical reference) to make the point (explain the idea). The caption, (state caption), includes the persuasive technique (identify persuasive technique – see Units 15–20). The visual makes an emotive appeal to our sense of (identify emotive appeal – see Unit 18) and projects a tone of (identify tone – see Unit 20). Readers are given the impression that (explain what message about the topic/issue readers may take from the image).

**b** Using the skeleton paragraph above as model, write a paragraph about the second cartoon, 'consume-survive'.

**Advertising** is one of the major features of popular culture. Overtly directed at the audience, advertising reaches most people in the community, affirming what is already valuable in their lives and offering direction on what ought to become important in their world.

Advertising text can be analysed in the same way as more traditional text. The table below provides a possible outline for this process.

| | |
|---|---|
| Purpose | What is the purpose of the advertisement? What does the advertiser hope to achieve? Is this explicit? |
| Audience | What is the target audience (age, gender, culture, lifestyle)? Who are the imagined users of the product that is advertised? Is there another potential audience? |
| Authority/source | What/who is the source of the advertisement? What/who is the assumed authority on the product? |
| Design | What choices do you think would have been made about the design of the advertisement and about what to put in and what to leave out? Are there any signs or symbols in the advertisement? What is their use designed to achieve? |
| Values | What are some of the explicit values and attitudes assumed to be shared by the readers/viewers? |
| Assumptions | What are some of the more implicit or taken-for-granted points of consensus, e.g. in relation to class, gender or generation? |
| Common features | What continuities and discontinuities are there across the range of advertisements? |

**To be successful, advertising has to appeal to its audience. The following are some commonly used appeals.**

**1** Appeals to authority

- → Celebrity endorsement: implies that by purchasing the endorsed product consumers can achieve the attractive aspects of the celebrity's character or situation.
- → Scientific claim: provides some sort of scientific proof or experiment, or an impressive sounding mystery ingredient. Claims are often made by people in white coats in laboratories or medical settings.
- → Rhetorical question: poses a question to the consumer that may be answered only in a product-affirming way.
- → Decisiveness: links the product with images of strength and positive decision-making by consumers.
- → Comparison: uses statements such as 'Double the strength of the old powder!'

**2** Appeals to personal considerations

- → Compliments/flattery: purchase of the product is an indication that a good decision has been made by a clever consumer.
- → Beauty: is attractive and draws the audience to beautiful people, places and objects
- → Care: appeals to parental (paternal or maternal) instincts and links products with protecting/caring impulses.
- → Approval: uses pressure by linking product use with friendship/acceptance.

**3** Appeals to social considerations

- → Lifestyle: links the product with a particular style of living or approach to life.
- → Conformity: associates products with behaviours or lifestyles that conform to or oppose society's norms and expectations.
- → Escape: appeals to the adventurous consumer; to the traveller who likes to get away from it all. The very idea of an escape from the pressures and deadlines of the everyday is appealing.

Look carefully at this advertisement.

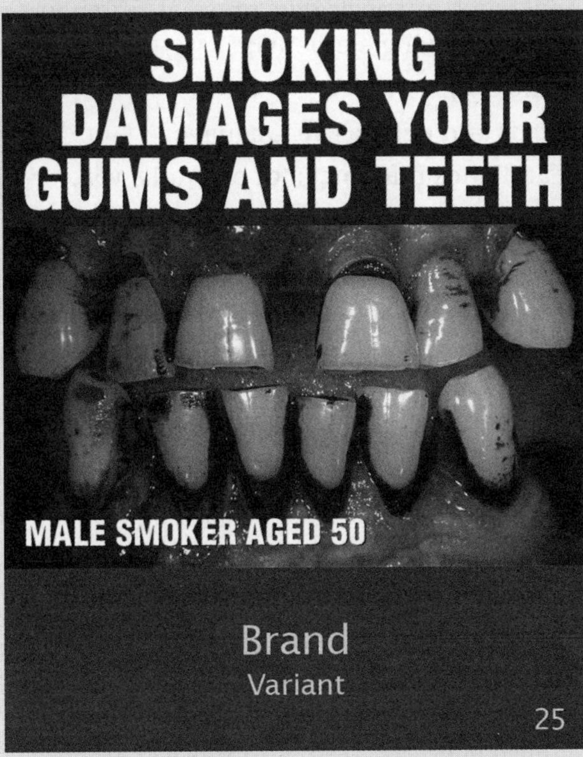


Health warning graphic © Professor Laurence J Walsh, The University of Queensland

Compile an analysis table for the advertisement.

| | |
|---|---|
| Purpose | |
| Audience | |
| Authority/source | |
| Design | |
| Values | |
| Assumptions | |
| Common features | |
| Appeals | |

**1** In your workbook, draw a cartoon expressing your comment on a matter of public interest. Incorporate symbolism, visual association or metaphorical reference. Include a caption or a punchline.

**2** In your workbook, create your own written magazine/newspaper classified advertisement for an event at your school (such as sports day, musical, art show or speech night). Your advertisement will need the following elements:

- a slogan advertising the event
- some emotional appeals and persuasive language
- inclusion of a direct audience reference; for example, *you*.

## SPELLING FOCUS

The words below are associated with the work that you have done in this unit. Many of them are part of the metalanguage of English. Make sure you can spell them all. Test yourself or work with a partner and test each other.

| | | | |
|---|---|---|---|
| anthropomorphism | authority | commentary | advertising |
| homogeneity | caricature | metaphorical | consensus |
| stereotype | humorous | advertisement | implicit |
| persuasive | cartoon | celebrity | in list twice |
| homogeneous | interpretation | endorsement | design |
| stereotypical | symbolism | advertiser | |
| behavioural | cartoonist | commercial | |
| humour | metaphor | explicit | |

Name: | Due date: | Guardian signature:

# 29 ELECTRONIC TEXTS

The grammar of reading, writing and viewing texts

From a reader's perspective it is important to remember that there is little control exercised over what is 'published' on the Internet or over who 'publishes' it, and that there is no mechanism in place to ensure accuracy or reliability of content. Even if what you are reading is accurate today, there is no guarantee that the website will still be there next time you wish to use it.

Avoid **screensucking** – spending more time in front of the computer than the task merits. The volume of material available to the researcher or casual visitor means that you have to be extremely well organised in your use of various **search engines** and **bookmarks** and in the **transfer of files**.

Indications of the **reliability** of your web source may be found in the contents and structure of the web page itself. Most web pages have a **header** and **footer** and within these you will usually find information about the author, institution and date of creation/revision.

The content and design of the page itself will provide evidence of **purpose** and **audience**.

The **language** of the page will also provide you with pointers as to purpose and audience. Is the language **formal** or **informal**? Is the **vocabulary** simple and limited, or sophisticated and extensive?

There are a number of procedures and questions to help you read and evaluate a website. **CACAO** is one example:

→ **Currency:** Is the site up-to-date?
→ **Authority:** Who compiled it? Who sponsors it?
→ **Coverage:** Does it contain appropriate material? Is the site easy to navigate?
→ **Accuracy:** Are other sources listed and, where appropriate, linked? Is there a full bibliography?
→ **Objectivity:** Is the site affiliated with any particular organisation or group? Is the viewpoint clear?

Not all websites are equally reliable.

**1** Find an example of each of the following.

a An Australian government website (one with '.gov.au' in its URL)

b An Australian educational website (one with '.edu.au' in its URL)

c A commercial website advertising clothing for young people (one with '.com' in its URL)

**2** Answer these exercises.

a Is the vocabulary of the government website straightforward or complex?

b Is the vocabulary of the government website informative or persuasive?

c Is the layout of the government website user-friendly? Did you find it easy to navigate?

d Is the vocabulary of the educational website straightforward or complex?

e Is the vocabulary of the educational website informative or persuasive?

f Is the layout of the educational website user-friendly? Did you find it easy to navigate?

g Is the vocabulary of the commercial website straightforward or complex?

h Is the vocabulary of the commercial website informative or persuasive?

i Is the layout of the commercial website user-friendly? Did you find it easy to navigate?

## EMAILS

Emails are both personal and workplace documents.

As personal documents, emails may be written informally using e-language (txt-language), reflecting the author's individual voice and style. Text may include acronyms – pronounceable words formed from the initial letters of other words (e.g. *LOL* = *laugh out loud*); initialisms – shortened forms of a phrase using the first letter of each word, which cannot be pronounced as a word on its own (e.g. *BTW* = *by the way*); or abbreviations – shortened forms of a single word or phrase that uses several letters of the word(s) (e.g. *XLNT* = *excellent*).

Emoticons may also be incorporated into the email text – these are 'pictures' made from punctuation marks depicting facial emotions when rotated (e.g. *:)* = *smile*). The choice of text font may assist in conveying tone and personality. Emojis are used in the same way as emoticons, but are pictures.

As workplace documents, emails have a formal style and follow standard language and letter conventions. They are structured like a letter – with a greeting, brief body paragraph(s) and a signature. The subject line summarises the content or purpose; the opening sentence does this also with some elaboration. Key information is presented concisely; additional information is mentioned succinctly. Finally, the writer indicates whether any action or reply is required. The content is relevant to the workplace context and must observe the codes of conduct of the workplace. The use of attachment documents and the inclusion of links enable emails to achieve some complexity. There are netiquette protocols concerning electronic communication, such as avoiding 'flaming' (abusive personal attacks) and 'shouting' (writing in capital letters). Email authors should not assume the privacy of their email and must be wary of defamatory comments.

## BLOGS

Blogs have the potential to combine text, visual effects, sound and graphics to convey ideas. There are two main styles of blogs – journalistic and personal – although features of these may be blended.

Journalistic blogs contain reports and commentary on public affairs. The text is usually presented in short block paragraphs and the content is structured in the inverted pyramid format (see Unit 33). The headlines and subheadings are informative and descriptive. Content may be presented in bullet points, boxes and links. Journalistic blogs use statement sentences with one idea per sentence, as well as the active voice, verbs and strong nouns to convey a lively journalistic voice. As blog readers tend to skim read, the text needs to utilise keywords and be in clearly identified small information packages. Generally, traditional language conventions are used. Journalistic blogs may be covered by legislation concerning defamation and slander, as well as journalistic codes of practice.

Personal blogs reflect the day-to-day life of the author and have a distinct individual voice. They often read like personal journals about thoughts and feelings. A conversational style and tone is fairly common. Traditional language conventions are not applied consistently. Acronyms, abbreviations, initialisms, emoticons or emojis may be incorporated in the text.

**1** You work in an office and you have received the following telephone message from your boss. Compose the emails as requested in the email templates on the next page.

E-texts are changing the way in which language is used.

I think the best thing to do would be to hold meetings for each person who will be affected by the first round of changes to the company structure. As I remember it, this would be Peter McGowan, Martin Bosco and Jacquie Waters. They should meet individually with Joachim Davente. Those involved in stage two changes, which is the entire third floor, should attend a series of information seminars on the 14th, 16th and 18th of this month, to be delivered by the change management group. It is important that all staff be given the opportunity to have some input on these occasions. I would also like to set up some small work groups, which would manage change in their immediate physical environment as well as to the systems and processes they use.

Could you send out a general email for all staff, informing them of the general picture? I think it's also important that those I've mentioned are contacted directly with details of their program.

As usual, I'll leave the actual organisation and composition of the communication to you. Thanks.

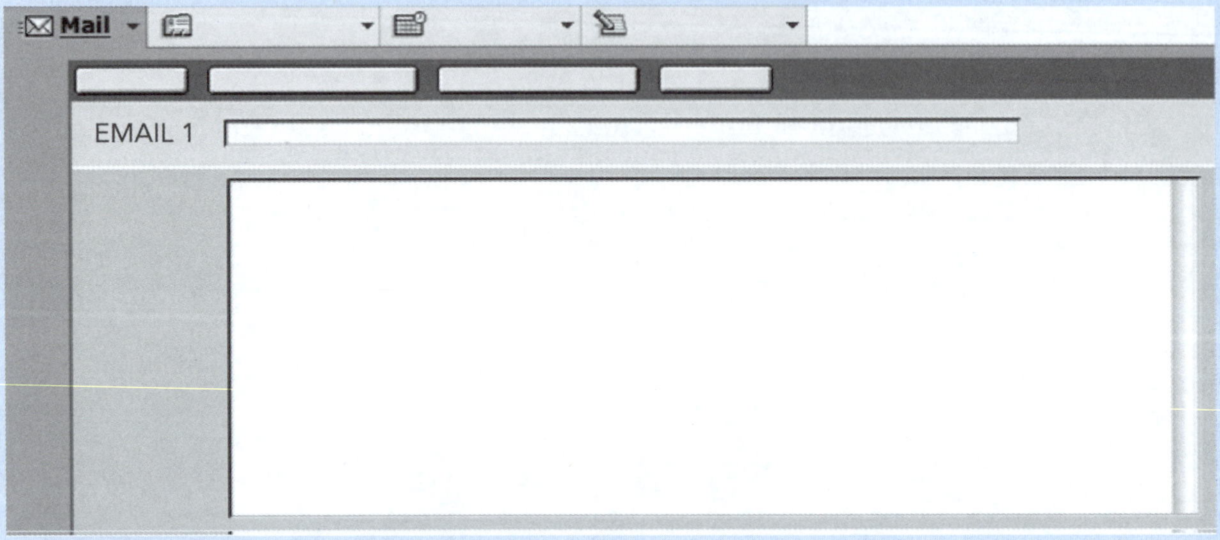

Mail

EMAIL 1

Mail

EMAIL 2

The words below are associated with your work in this unit. Many of them are part of the metalanguage of English. Make sure you can spell them all. Test yourself or work with a partner and test each other.

| acronym | emoji | concise | netiquette | graphics |
|---|---|---|---|---|
| emoticon | informal | formal | defamatory | succinct |

| Name: | Due date: | Guardian signature: |
|---|---|---|

# 30 GRAPHIC TEXTS

The grammar of reading, writing and viewing texts

Graphic texts are popular and cover a range of genres – from fiction and nonfiction to adaptations and modernised versions of classic literature. Graphic novels contain some of the basic features found in other types of texts – especially narrative-based texts such as novels, short stories, ballads, plays, films and comics. These basic features include elements such as narrative structure, setting and context, characterisation, dialogue, themes, ideas, issues and genre. Additionally, graphic novels have their own features and conventions. This includes visual elements like text and graphics, and also visual style, which refers to the conventions of the chosen artistic style.

Discussing the construction elements of a graphic text requires specific metalanguage. Some of this metalanguage comes from the features of literary texts, but much of it comes from film terminology, as well as from artistic features and concepts. The table below lists some of the key metalanguage.

| | | |
|---|---|---|
| Framing/shots: establishing shot, long shot, medium shot, close-up, extreme close-up | Framing/angles: low, direct, high, bird's eye view | Transitions (changes between cells) |
| *Mise-en-scène* (composition) | Colour and shading | Font style |
| Line thickness | Point-of-view framing | Over-the-shoulder point of view framing |
| Juxtaposition | Visual symbol or image | Recurring visual motif |
| Artistic style (e.g. realistic, fantasy, comic etc.) | Lighting: direct lighting, indirect lighting | Montage |
| Voice over narration | Cell or panel | Borderless panel |
| Splash | Emanate | Speech bubble |
| Caricature | Blurring | Comic strip format |
| Thought cloud | Icon | Gutter |
| Foreground | Midground | Background |

Recent popular graphic novels include: *The Arrival* by Shaun Tan, *Fun Home: A Family Tragicomic* by Alison Bechdel, *The Complete Maus* by Art Spiegelman, and *Persepolis* by Marjane Satrapi. Classical literature such as *The Hobbit* and many of William Shakespeare's plays have been adapted into graphic texts.

**1** Read the extract from 'Romeo and Juliet', a graphic text adaptation of the play by William Shakespeare. The play tells the tragedy of teenage lovers, Romeo and Juliet, who defy their parents and run away to elope. A series of rash decisions, coincidences and conflicts leads to an intense catastrophic conclusion. The play is an exploration of love and hate, youth and age, and fate and destiny. The scene below illustrates the famous "balcony scene", where the pair declare their love.

**Most cartoons use a combination of written and visual text.**

AY ME!
SHE SPEAKS: O, SPEAK AGAIN, BRIGHT ANGEL!
FOR THOU ART AS GLORIOUS TO THIS NIGHT, BEING O'ER MY HEAD, AS IS A WINGED MESSENGER OF HEAVEN UNTO THE WHITE-UPTURNED WOND'RING EYES OF MORTALS, THAT FALL BACK TO GAZE ON HIM, WHEN HE BESTRIDES THE LAZY-PACING CLOUDS AND SAILS UPON THE BOSOM OF THE AIR.
O ROMEO, ROMEO!
WHEREFORE ART THOU ROMEO?
DENY THY FATHER, AND REFUSE THY NAME: OR, IF THOU WILT NOT, BE BUT SWORN MY LOVE, AND I'LL NO LONGER BE A CAPULET.
SHALL I HEAR MORE, OR SHALL I SPEAK AT THIS?
'TIS BUT THY NAME THAT IS MY ENEMY: THOU ART THYSELF THOUGH, NOT A MONTAGUE.
WHAT'S MONTAGUE?
IT IS NOT HAND, NOR FOOT, NOR ARM, NOR FACE, NOR ANY OTHER PART BELONGING TO A MAN.
O! BE SOME OTHER NAME.
WHAT'S IN A NAME? THAT WHICH WE CALL A ROSE, BY ANY OTHER WORD WOULD SMELL AS SWEET;
SO ROMEO WOULD, WERE HE NOT ROMEO CALL'D, RETAIN THAT DEAR PERFECTION WHICH HE OWES, WITHOUT THAT TITLE.
ROMEO, DOFF THY NAME; AND FOR THY NAME, WHICH IS NO PART OF THEE, TAKE ALL MYSELF!
I TAKE THEE AT THY WORD. CALL ME BUT LOVE, AND I'LL BE NEW BAPTIS'D;
HENCEFORTH I NEVER WILL BE ROMEO.
WHAT MAN ART THOU, THAT, THUS BESCREEN'D IN NIGHT, SO STUMBLEST ON MY COUNSEL?


 

**a** Can you identify the visual elements of a graphic text? Identify and annotate key graphic text features in the extract from 'Romeo and Juliet'.

**b** How does the graphic artist use particular features to convey the relationship between Romeo and Juliet?

**c** What atmosphere is conveyed? Select a graphic feature that conveys this atmosphere.

**1** Visit your school library or local library. Browse through the Graphic Texts section and select a graphic text to read. Read the text.

**2** When you have read the graphic text, complete the following responses.

**a** Where is the narrative set (e.g. place/location; interior/exterior)?

**b** When does the narrative take place: time period (e.g. day/afternoon/night), season?

**c** From whose point of view is the narrative told?

**d** Who are the main characters – give names and three adjectives for each to describe what they are like?

**e** What is the central conflict/problem/challenge in the narrative?

**f** What is/are the sub-conflicts in the narrative?

**g** What are the main events in the narrative?

**h** What is the climax of the narrative?

**i** What is the resolution?

**j** Quote a significant visual symbol or image from the narrative. What ideas does it suggest?

**k** Is there a dominant pattern in the visual organisation of the text?

**l** Note a significant visual element in the text and explain its purpose.

**m** Note an interesting cell and comment on its framing and/or angle.

**n** Describe the overall visual style of the text.

**o** How would you define the genre of the text?

**p** What do you think is the main theme, idea or issue in the narrative?

**q** What is the significance of the text's title?

**r** How is the reader left thinking and feeling about the text?

**s** Give this text a recommend rating out of 5 and justify your rating. (where 0 = not recommended and 5 = highly recommended) ____________________

**SPELLING FOCUS**

The words below are associated with the work that you have done in this unit. Many of them are part of the metalanguage of English. Make sure you can spell them all. Test yourself or work with a partner and test each other.

| | | | |
|---|---|---|---|
| transition | juxtaposition | motif | caricature |
| *mise-en-scène* | visual | montage | |

Name:

Due date:

Guardian signature:

# 31 THE SPEECH

The grammar of reading, writing and viewing texts

Whenever you are required to make an oral presentation, you will be reassured if you recognise that the audience is on your side and that most speakers, like you, are learning the art of public presentations and public speaking. It may also help to think of your task not so much in terms of 'making a **speech**', as of 'talking to your audience'. This will help you establish a strong connection with your listeners as well as making you less nervous. You should attempt to maintain audience engagement by continuing to speak to its members and maintaining eye contact with them.

Although your audience is likely to be sympathetic, this is no excuse for failing to prepare adequately. At all times you must be conscious of the nature of your **audience** as well as your **purpose** in presenting; your manner and vocabulary will change according to these aspects.

In addition, you must consider the **physical setting** of your presentation; you cannot expect an audience to listen actively if it is either unable to hear what you have to say or if you shout. It is up to you to ensure that your voice is **audible** (speak out to your audience, not down to your cue cards); that your **delivery** is appropriately paced (i.e. not too fast); and that what you are saying is readily understood (**clearly enunciated**). In addition, it is important to **research** your topic and **organise** the content appropriately. You should decide whether to use a slide presentation program. If you do choose to use such assistance, ensure that you use it to signpost the content of your presentation or to add supportive material such as relevant photographs, illustrations and diagrams. Never simply type your presentation into the program and then read the same text from a piece of paper.

**Organisation** includes a clear statement of your topic or contention, an outline of your major points (signposting) and a logical progression from one point to the next. You must include **evidence** in support of your point of view, which can take the form of external evidence (statistics, quotes from experts and so on), or anecdotal evidence, especially if it is likely to be directly relevant to your audience. It may mirror their experience, it may be a particularly powerful or moving story or it may call on them to participate actively in response to it. An appropriately amusing or poignant anecdote is an excellent way to begin or end a presentation, again because it is a very powerful tool for **engaging** your audience. Make sure you practise your presentation so you know the content and can gauge its length, remembering that you are likely to speak more quickly in a public forum than you do ordinarily.

Being positive, enthusiastic and well organised in any presentation will enable you to engage your audience. Excellent content and appropriate delivery will assist in maintaining that involvement. After all, the main purpose of a public presentation is to present your material and have it received thoughtfully.

**1** On 5 September 1942, Australian author Miles Franklin delivered a tribute to the poet and short-story writer Henry Lawson, on the occasion of the unveiling of a statue of Lawson in Sydney. Read the following extract from her speech, then answer the questions.

Good speeches use language differently from the language of written texts.

… First among Lawson's achievements was the embodying of the tradition of mateship.

Second, he was one of the most powerful of that band which in the 'nineties helped Australians to a realisation of their country. He quickened their instinctive reaction towards it … Henry Lawson lighted lamps for us in a vast and lonely habitat. He recalled the far-flung homesickness of the generations which had remained exiled. He made them see … the grand new discovery of our own sun, to see it setting red and real and near at hand … Henry Lawson gave us this kingdom for our own, wove it so that we could feel it around ourselves with the comfort of a blanket …

I never saw Henry Lawson again. I too left Australia and when I returned the earth – that Australian earth cleansed of history by an oblivion of fallow-hood – lay kind upon him who had helped to give it national significance …

Our indebtedness to him will increase because he has rendered this continent. He has helped to make Australia ours in a way that no system of land exploitation, nor even droughts and floods and pests, can take it from us – a great gift from a greatly gifted man – Henry Lawson.

Speech given by Miles Franklin at the Henry Lawson Statue, Sydney, NSW on 5 September 1942.
Published in Meanjin papers No. 12 Dec. 1942. State Library of NSW [MLMSS 3639].

**a** What is the purpose and audience of Franklin's speech?

**b** What is its tone?

**c** What signposting can you find? What is its effect?

**d** What is Franklin's view of Australia, as expressed here?

**2** The following consists of extracts from a speech delivered at Redfern on 10 December 1992 by then Australian Prime Minister, Paul Keating. Read the speech, then answer the questions that follow.

More I think than most Australians recognise, the plight of Aboriginal Australians affects us all …

That is perhaps the point of this Year of the World's Indigenous People: to bring the dispossessed out of the shadows, to recognise that they are part of us, and that we cannot give Indigenous Australians up without giving up many of our own most deeply held values, much of our own identity – and our own humanity …

We non-Aboriginal Australians should perhaps remind ourselves that Australia once reached out for us …

Isn't it reasonable to say that if we can build a prosperous and remarkably harmonious multicultural society in Australia, surely we can find just solutions to the problems which beset the first Australians – the people to whom the most injustice has been done.

And, as I say, the starting point might be to recognise that the problem starts with us non-Aboriginal Australians. It begins, I think, with that act of recognition. Recognition that it was we who did the dispossessing. We took the traditional lands and smashed the traditional way of life. We brought the diseases. The alcohol. We committed the murders. We took the children from their mothers.

We practised discrimination and exclusion. It was our ignorance and our prejudice. And our failure to imagine these things being done to us. With some noble exceptions, we failed to make the most basic human response and enter into their hearts and minds. We failed to ask: how would I feel if this were done to me? As a consequence, we failed to see that what we were doing degraded all of us ...

Where Aboriginal Australians have been included in the life of Australia, they have made remarkable contributions ... they have shaped our knowledge of this continent and of ourselves. They have shaped our identity. They are there in the Australian legend. We should never forget – they have helped build this nation. And if we have a sense of justice, as well as common sense, we will forge a new partnership. As I said, it might help us if we non-Aboriginal Australians imagined ourselves dispossessed of land we had lived on for fifty thousand years – and then imagined ourselves told that it had never been ours. Imagine if ours was the oldest culture in the world and we were told that it was worthless. Imagine if we had resisted this settlement, suffered and died in the defence of our land, and then were told in history books that we had given up without a fight. Imagine if non-Aboriginal Australians had served their country in peace and war and were then ignored in history books. Imagine if our feats on sporting fields had inspired admiration and patriotism and yet did nothing to diminish prejudice. Imagine if our spiritual life was denied and ridiculed. Imagine if we had suffered the injustice and then were blamed for it. It seems to me that if we can imagine the injustice, we can imagine its opposite. And we can have justice ...

There is one thing today we cannot imagine. We cannot imagine that the descendants of people whose genius and resilience maintained a culture here through fifty thousand years or more, through cataclysmic changes to the climate and environment, and who then survived two centuries of dispossession and abuse, will be denied their place in the modern Australian nation. We cannot imagine that. We cannot imagine that we will fail.

Keating, P 2012, Redfern Address, Commonwealth of Australia (National Archives of Australia), 2012.

**a** What is the purpose and audience of Keating's speech?

**b** What is its tone?

**c** Identify the speech elements used. Are they effective?

**d** Underline uses of repetition. What is the effect of these?

**e** How does the view of Australia expressed by Keating contrast with that expressed by Franklin? How might you account for that difference?

**1** Create and present a short persuasive speech on one of the following topics. You will need to do some research. Incorporate a range of persuasive language devices into your speech.

- → 'Blood sports should be banned.' Discuss.
- → Advertising: good or bad?
- → 'Students should not pay full public transport fares until they turn 18 years old.' Discuss.
- → Summer or winter: which do you prefer?
- → Should Australia become a republic?
- → Honesty or dishonesty: which is better?
- → Are wars ever necessary?
- → 'All forms of gambling should be banned.' Discuss.
- → 'Australian capital cities should have permanent water restrictions.' What do you think?
- → 'There should be more marine reserves in Australia.' What do you think?
- → 'All teenagers should obey an evening curfew.' Agree or disagree?
- → 'Our criminal sentencing system is failing the victims of crime.' Discuss.
- → 'Electronic media are better than books.' What do you think?
- → Vegetarianism or carnivorism: which is better?
- → 'Computers have improved the world.' Discuss.

**2** Find a speech that you like (many are available on the Internet).

**a** What is its appeal for you?

**b** What speech elements can you identify?

**c** Is there any aspect of the speech that you would use in future presentations of your own?

## SPELLING FOCUS

The words below are associated with the work that you have done in this unit. Make sure you can spell them all. Test yourself or work with a partner and test each other.

| anecdotal | enunciated | progression | contention | organisation |
|---|---|---|---|---|
| audible | inaudible | anecdote | enunciation | research |

| Name: | Due date: | Guardian signature: |
|---|---|---|
| | | |

# 32 THE NONFICTION TEXT

The grammar of reading, writing and viewing texts

Non-fiction texts incorporate a range of journalistic forms of writing, one of which is the **feature article**. There are two broad categories of features.

→ **News features** are based on current affairs. They may provide background information, an overview of opinions, an explanation about a situation/process and analysis/commentary. News features may be investigative in their approach – that is, they may outline causes, consequences and solutions – or they may build a case for or against an issue or situation.

→ **Entertainment features** cover areas of general public interest – from travel to sports; from the arts to philosophical matters. Human-interest features enable readers to gain in-depth knowledge of a particular subject (usually a high-profile public figure).

The classic feature article has a focus theme and some key ingredients: facts, quotes, examples, descriptions and anecdotes. There are several common structures used to build a feature:

→ **News-story form:** the **'inverted pyramid'** structure – that is, information about who, what, where, when, why and how is organised from the most important to the least important

→ **Narrative form:** a combination of news-story form features and fiction writing features (such as description, dialogue and anecdotes)

→ **Question–answer form:** a series of questions and answers

→ **List form:** lists of facts, figures or ideas on a specific topic

Generally, features are written in a formal style, but a conversational style may be used to reflect the unique style and tone of the writer. Normally, sentences are succinct. Words and phrases are concrete and direct – subject-specific vocabulary and/or concepts may be incorporated. Evocative adjectives and lively verbs are used to build descriptions. Writers often weave thematic connotations into a range of words and phrases.

**1** Read this feature article and complete the questions that follow.

## BIGGEST SQUAD EVER

The biggest squad ever to go to the Paralympics from Australia has been chosen for the London Summer Paralympics. The team of 161 athletes is expected to continue Australia's outstanding performance in previous games. There are high hopes that the team will finish in the top five, as it has done since the games in Atlanta in 1996. President of the Australian Paralympic Committee, Greg Hartung, said, 'The APC believes this Team is well prepared to take on the challenge.'

The London Paralympics will be the biggest and most competitive games yet held, with 4200 athletes from 160 countries. It is the 15th Paralympics and will be held between 29 August and 9 September 2012.

Australians have competed in every Paralympics since the games were established in Rome in 1960. Our biggest team ever will be competing in 13 different sports. About half the team is attending a Paralympic competition for the first time, but they are led by some well-known champions. Wheelchair racer Kurt Fearnley is confident of winning his third gold Olympic medal in the Wheelchair Marathon. If he achieves his dream, he will be the first athlete to win three consecutive marathons. Super-fish Matt Cowdrey has a long list of medals to his name, since his debut as an 18-year-old in Athens, where he won five gold, two silver and one bronze. At the Beijing Games he captained the Paralympic team, winning five gold and three silver medals – a bigger tally than any other competitor at those games. In London he will be competing in an astonishing eight different events – 100 m breaststroke, 50 m freestyle, 100 m freestyle, 100 m backstroke, 200 m individual medley, 4 × 100 m medley relay, 100 m butterfly and 4 × 100 m freestyle.

The veteran of the Australian team is the amazing Libby Kosmala, who will be both Australia's oldest competitor and the oldest competitor at the Games. The 70-year-old South Australian will be competing in her 11th Paralympics. She first competed at Heidleberg in 1972. Born a paraplegic, Kosmala's chosen sport is shooting. She has won nine gold medals. Her greatest triumph was at the 1984 Games when she won four gold medals and broke four world records in air rifle shooting. Kosmala said that the equipment has changed for the better over the years. 'The rifles are more accurate now,' Kosmala said. 'We now have

Feature articles often provide background to news articles.

electronic targets with immediate scores next to us but also the athlete holding the rifle has to be extremely accurate as well.'

One difference between the Paralympics and the Olympics is the use of classification to ensure fair competition. In the same way as in most competitions men only compete against other men or lightweight boxers only compete against athletes of the same weight, athletes are classified according to the way in which their disability is an impairment to their performance in a particular sport. The rules are different for each sport as every sport requires different skills and competencies.

All great athletes are inspiring, but there is something special about the determination and dedication of our Paralympic athletes as they prepare for another triumph in London.

Adapted from 'PM launches 2012 Australian Paralympic Media', by APC Media, posted 25 June 2012 (www.paralympic.org.au) and from 'Kosmala on target for 11th Games', *ABC News*, 22 May 2012.

**a** Which category does this feature article fall into?

**b** What is the focus theme of this article?

**c** Can you discern the writer's point of view?

**d** List instances of the following from the article.

**i** Facts

**ii** Examples

**iii** Quotations

**iv** Words with positive connotations that show the writer's opinion

**v** Background information that the reader might need to understand the topic

**2** You have been reading a feature article. The following, which contains a lot of the same material, is a news article. How are the two articles different?

## PARALYMPIC TEAM ANNOUNCED

Greg Hartung, President of the Australian Paralympic Committee, announced today the names of the 161 athletes who will go to London to represent Australia in the 2012 Summer Paralympics.

'The APC believes this Team is well prepared for the challenge,' he said.

Among the athletes named are veterans such as wheelchair racer Kurt Fearnley and super-fish Matt Cowdrey. Fearnley is hoping to win his third gold Olympic medal in the Wheelchair Marathon. Cowdrey, who has a stack of medals to his name, will be competing in eight different events.

The oldest member of the team is shooter Libby Kosmala. At 70 years old, Kosmala will also be the oldest competitor at the London Paralympics.

About half the team is attending a Paralympic competition for the first time, the APC president said.

Construct a profile feature article based on an individual of your choice. Your profile should combine factual information about the person as well as an exposé of something unique or interesting about their life. Complete the following exercises to construct your article.

**1** Brainstorm a list of useful questions to gain biographical information and to learn about a unique or interesting aspect of the person's life. Ask open-ended questions that elicit an explanatory response, rather than yes/no answers. Be prepared to follow up leads if your subject reveals some interesting material.

**2** Make notes about major points that arise in the interview. Check details for accuracy. Be respectful – don't ask about private matters.

**3** Review your material and make decisions about selection of content. Determine the focus of your article. Write this in a sentence below.

**4** Write your profile feature article in your workbook or type it onto a computer. You may begin with an introductory paragraph and continue in question–answer format.

**SPELLING FOCUS**

The words below are associated with the work that you have done in this unit. Many of them are part of the metalanguage of English. Make sure you can spell them all. Test yourself or work with a partner and test each other.

| | | | | |
|---|---|---|---|---|
| analysis | evocative | succinct | current | investigation |
| connotation | feature | commentary | explanation | vocabulary |

Name: | Due date: | Guardian signature:

# 33 THE COMPARATIVE LITERATURE RESPONSE

The grammar of responding to texts

Comparative literature responses are an exciting opportunity to explore texts within a different framework. Comparing two texts enables you to demonstrate your understanding of both texts (and of text types in general) in a broader and yet more complex way. To compare/contrast texts it is important that you build up a detailed and well-supported analysis of each text before you re-read them with comparison in mind.

Read the relevant units in the section 'The grammar of reading, writing and viewing texts' carefully and ensure you have covered all necessary areas in relation to each text. You may choose to do this in note/subheading form, mind map, table etc. The most important thing is that you have a written record of key features and strategies as the foundation.

The examples used here are from David Malouf's *Fly Away Peter* and Stephen Crane's *The Red Badge of Courage*. The analyses are incomplete and would require additional work and much more detail if you were studying either novel. Each example is presented in a different format.

## *FLY AWAY PETER*

### FEATURE: THEMES

| Examples | Quotes | Comment |
|---|---|---|
| Jim Saddler's journey from Australia (New World) to the battlefields of Europe (Old World) and what it means | pp. 36, 55 World tilting towards Europe<br>p. 33 'Europe … a mad place' | Senses the need to touch something momentous and to see it with his own eyes<br>Sense of place established through natural world, so dislocation in Europe at mercy of death on industrial scale almost total<br>Re-establishes sense of self through once again naming birds he sees |
| Exploration of identity – Jim's and Australia's | p. 64 J 'wondered about himself' | |
| Exploration of ideas of boundaries – national, class, individual | p. 85 Eric's fundamental question 'about the structure of the world … and where they belonged in it…and who had power over them… | |
| Search for meaning in an individual's life and/or death | p. 132 'A life wasn't for anything. It simply was.' | |
| Proceeds through a set of binary oppositions: | p. 103 'dangerous innocence' | |
| New World → Old<br>Innocence → experience | p. 100 'feel immeasurably old'<br>pp. 68–9 Egypt comparison | |
| Natural world machinery of war | p. 76 war entered through a 'gap in a hedge'<br>p. 104 'It was annihilating. It was all.' | |
| Permanence → transience | p. 106 'It was time for winter sowing'<br>J '[finds] his way back to a natural cycle of things … undisturbed'<br>p. 61 'stories of a life… elsewhere… the birds' | |
| Individual action → collective action | p. 64 J 'wondered about himself' | |

## FEATURE: NARRATIVE VIEWPOINT

| Examples | Quotes | Comment |
|---|---|---|
| 3rd person participant narrator established as acute observer from the beginning | | Country boy with very strong sense of place<br>Historically accurate voice and vocabulary<br>Momentous events seen through individual's eyes<br>Example of fate of many young Australian men in WWI<br>Established as acute observer from the beginning |

## FEATURE: CHARACTERS

| Examples | Quotes | Comment |
|---|---|---|
| Jim Saddler | He moved always on these two levels | Long view to close-up |
| Ashleigh | | |
| Imogen | | |
| Clancy<br>Whizzer<br>Eric } | Force Jim to confront reality of war, death and inequality | |
| Jim's father | Individual violence<br>Jim forced to recognise seeds of that same violence in himself in the war | |

## FEATURE: STRUCTURE

| Examples | Quotes | Comment |
|---|---|---|
| Short novel (novella)<br>2 distinct sections/settings<br>Journey of Jim from Australia (New World) to battlefields of Europe (Old World)<br>Proceeds through set of binary opposites:<br>New World → Old<br>Innocence → experience<br>Natural world → machinery of war<br>Permanence → transience<br>Life → death<br>Individual action → collective action | | Part 1<br>Establishes the reality of Australian landscape<br>Primacy of natural world and continuity<br>Establishes characters of J, A and I and the basis of their interaction (natural world)<br>Part 2<br>Established as the geographical and philosophical opposite of Australia |

## FEATURE: STYLE AND SYMBOLISM

| Examples | Quotes | Comment |
|---|---|---|
| Follows journey of young Australian man from a bird sanctuary in SE Qld to the Western Front in WWI<br>Other characters force him to reflect on life and how he interacts with it<br>Use of landscape/nature as symbols of continuity<br>Birds' migration echoes Jim's journey | | |
| Movement from periphery (Aus) to centre (Europe) – half migratory pattern of birds (Peter/Paul)<br>Importance of maps and mapping–Bi-plane | He moved always on these two levels | Long view to close-up |

## *THE RED BADGE OF COURAGE*

**THEMES**
- nature of courage
- war as industrial process
- individual vs collective action
- nature of death
- war and defining a nation
- innocence — experience
- what does it mean to be a man?

**CHARACTERS**
- Henry Fleming - the youth
- Jim Comklin - the tall soldier
- Wilson - Henry's young friend
- significance of names? lack of individual names

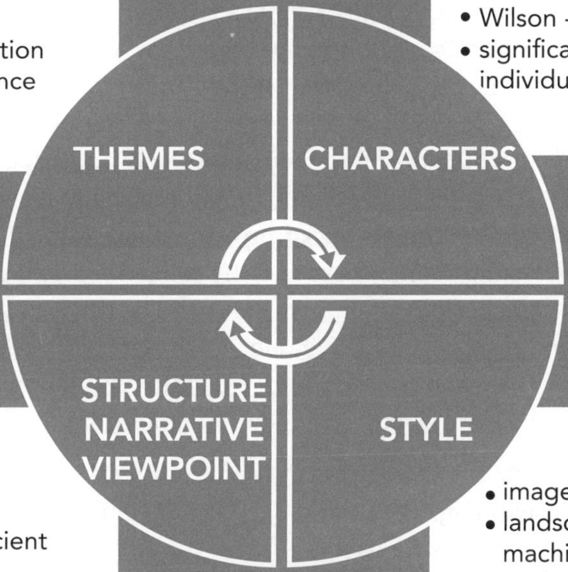

**STRUCTURE NARRATIVE VIEWPOINT**
- short novel
- short chapters
- 3rd person omniscient narrator

**STYLE**
- imagery and symbolism
- landscape/nature vs machinery of war
- gods, monsters and birds

In planning a response a student would build on this diagram to include page references and quotes to illustrate each of the points.

Choose one of the methodologies above (or one you have developed) and organise information on your two texts. Looking at the information in each analysis, it should be easier to see the points at which you can compare and contrast them. It would be useful to skim-read each text again with those points and the idea of comparison in mind. What are the common views? Are there differences and are there reasons for this?

The essay structure for this task is relatively straightforward. What you must not do is write a paragraph on the first text and then follow it with another paragraph on the second. Having developed readings, use the important ideas and structures as points of comparison, always ensuring that you are writing within the terms of the question; that is, you use them as your topic sentences in a series of paragraphs that directly compare the two texts. Remember that you may be given a rather general prompt for discussion or asked to respond to a specific question.

What are the major concerns of *Fly Away Peter* and *The Red Badge of Courage?*

## INTRODUCTION

Name the texts and authors you are discussing in your response

Respond directly to the question, setting out your point of view clearly

Outline your major points of comparison, making sure that they are relevant to the question.

Both novellas, David Malouf's *Fly Away Peter* and *The Red Badge of Courage* by Stephen Crane, deal with the journey of young men from innocence to experience; a journey which mirrors the development of each country's image of itself as a nation of the 'new world' forged in the crucible of war. Both involve protagonists who are young, naïve and generally overwhelmed by the complex and violent situations in which they find themselves. The landscape operates almost as a character in the books; functioning on realistic and symbolic levels – the continuous backdrop against which the individual dramas of the young country boys and the collective dramas of their compatriots are played out. In both cases the landscape is also the foundation image of complex and intricate symbolic structures. In each work, the reader is also presented with a small number of other characters who are significant; they stand out from the rest and illustrate points of view on life, death, courage and war.

**Paragraphs 1, 2 and 3:** points of comparison, discussion, examples and links for each

**Paragraph 4** (optional, depending on question): major point of contrast and link

## CONCLUSION

Re-statement of your major points

Comparison of Text 1 and Text 2

Contextualising statement

Although one is written in the 19th century and the other in the 20th, each novel examines the struggle of a young country to define itself, especially in relation to the extreme circumstances of war; in one case a debilitating and shattering civil war and in the other a horrendous conflict which arguably shook the European world's vision of its 'civilized' self. Through an intricate interweaving of individual and collective experiences in complex symbolic landscapes the truly shattering consequences of war are explored.

Remember that writing an analytical essay, comparative or otherwise, is a circular process. You begin with the text(s) break it/them into the relevant components for your discussion. Your conclusion should re-assemble the text(s) and present your view again in a holistic way.

On a separate piece of paper, complete an essay plan for the question below:

**a** 'Every text is in time and place, but the good ones transcend both.' Discuss with reference to two texts you have studied this year.

Name: | Due date: | Guardian signature:

# 34 THE CREATIVE RESPONSE TO LITERATURE

The grammar of responding to texts

A creative response to literature allows you to explore your understanding of a text and its context and tests your knowledge of the structures authors use to convey their views and to engage. You will need to complete a three-part process.

## PART 1: DEVELOP YOUR OWN READING

Exploring the structures and features of the text to develop your own reading is the first step. (See units in the section 'The grammar of reading, writing and viewing texts'.) It is crucial that you have an in-depth understanding of your chosen text.

You will need to consider the author's purpose, the audience, the text's context as well as your own – your experiences and knowledge form part of your response to the text and are vital in the production of your own text.

Make notes on the following aspects of your study text:

→ audience and purpose

→ structure – narrative viewpoint, mechanics of novel. How do the structures and features of the text convey and develop the themes?

→ themes/main ideas discussed, views of individual characters about these ideas

→ characters – major characters (including detailed character study). Are they named or described? Are they revealed by words or actions? How do they function in the text?

→ style – type of vocabulary used, imagery and symbolism

## PART 2: PLAN YOUR RESPONSE

Select the aspect of the text you want to explore and then decide how you are going to do that. Remember all texts are constructed to elicit a desired response so construct yours with that in mind.

Select a key scene, character, or idea worthy of further investigation and, bearing in mind the author's use of audience and purpose to create meaning, begin to work on your response.

You could compose a significant scene omitted from the original text; you might write a prequel or a sequel. You might choose to rewrite a scene as if it were seen by someone other than the narrator, such as the police officer in *The Curious Incident of the Dog in the Night-time*. Or you might reconstruct a scene in *Amadeus*, with Mozart as narrator rather than Salieri. In preparation you will need to make many decisions *before* you begin constructing your response.

## PART 3: WRITE AN EXPLANATION

Record every aspect of the choices you have made using the first person and addressing these questions:

→ What is my aim (purpose) in writing and for whom am I writing (audience)?

→ What form structure will my piece take? Why?

→ What is the appropriate language i.e. tone and vocabulary? How do I ensure consistency of voice and style? How can I adapt language and literary devices to generate particular responses from readers?

→ Have I made explicit the connection(s) between the text and my piece?

The stories in MacLeod's anthology, ***Island***, revolve around family relationships and memory. Write a creative response that explores these ideas.

Student understanding of the text

It seems to me that in his anthology, *Island*, Alistair MacLeod's short stories deal with the double-edged qualities of the way of life he describes. Family relationships and the role of memory which stand at the heart of his writing are supportive and organising factors in life while also being the elements capable of causing people's lives to unravel and families to fracture. In addition, I can see that these ideas are thrown into high relief by the remarkable Newfoundland landscape, which gives his short stories a magical quality. That landscape imparts a beauty almost beyond imagination, but it is also the bringer of tragedies to communities, families and individuals.

Student identifies a personal context

I don't know anything of the Canadian landscape, but my grandparents live in what most people would call 'the outback' where families and their support are essential to existence and where the landscape is the dominant force, dictating survival or otherwise.

Student identifies the form of the response

Student links their creative response to the text

Student explains the structure of the creative response

Student provides a direct thematic link to the text

I therefore decided to write a short story using MacLeod's ideas of family and memory and the power of landscape as the twin pillars of existence. The structure of the piece is an interaction between three elements: a photo album being examined by a great grandmother and the conversation between her and her great grandson who is visiting her on the family agricultural property in the outback. Through their discussion, it becomes clear that the boy is seeking to place himself in his family narrative and the woman is keen to reinforce the importance of memory in shaping such a family and the active role the landscape has played in the success or otherwise of their family enterprises. It may be beneficial, benign and beautiful, but it may equally be most dangerous when at its most magical.

Student identifies direct links to the text

Student provides a direct thematic link to the text

Student highlights the relationship between language choices and the creative response

Student identifies the purpose of the response

Student identifies the audience

While the language I have chosen to use is basically informal, it is important that the woman's vocabulary is indicative of her age, as are the vernacular terms used by the child. I have selected some of the 'older' words directly from MacLeod's stories, but I have updated the 'slang' used by the boy to make it clear that this is a contemporary Australian conversation, designed to explore Macleod's ideas in a context more familiar to the Year 12 readers at whom the short story is aimed.

**TAKE IT FURTHER**

Here are some examples of topics for creative responses. You may use these as actual questions or use the structure to form your own questions, relevant to your study texts.

**a** *Burial Rites* explores the notion that justice can never be absolute.

**b** *Frankenstein* explores the most fundamental dilemma of all: what it is to be human.

| Name: | Due date: | Guardian signature: |
|---|---|---|

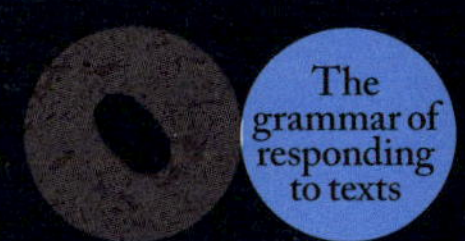


# REVISION TEST

**1** Complete the following word-family table to show that you know the difference between nouns, verbs, adverbs and adjectives.

| Noun | Verb | Adverb | Adjective |
|---|---|---|---|
| ability | | | |
| | abound | | |
| | | | bitterly |
| | | clear | |
| | | | deeply |
| education | | | |
| fire | | | |
| | injure | | |
| | | | lazily |
| | | moral | |

**2** **a** Underline the sentence in which the word *after* is used as a conjunction.

After he had finished work, he met some friends for coffee.

After work, he met some friends for coffee.

**b** Underline the sentence in which the word *since* is used as a conjunction.

I hadn't seen them since Christmas.

I hadn't seen them since they left at Christmas time.

**c** Underline the sentence in which the word *because* is used as a conjunction.

Because of the strike, we had to wait ages for a train.

Because there was a strike, we had to wait ages for a train.

**d** Underline the sentence in which the word *before* is used as a preposition.

I want to see you before class.

I want to see you before the bell rings for class.

**3** What part of speech is the italicised word in each of the following sentences?.

**a** *Who* is going to volunteer for this project? ______________________

**b** The person *who* volunteers first will win an award. ______________________

c Don't take that racquet. That's *mine*. ______

d *I* was confused. ______

**4** Underline the sentence in each pair below that contains a transitive verb.

a He was running fast.

He was running a new program.

b I don't like driving in foggy conditions.

I don't like driving his old van.

c She smiled at me.

She smiled an enigmatic smile.

**5** Underline the sentence in each pair below that contains a passive verb.

a The new proposals will be announced at the press conference.

The prime minister will announce the new proposals.

b Trespassers will be prosecuted.

Farmers in this district will prosecute trespassers.

c The students heated the mixture over a Bunsen burner.

The mixture was heated over a Bunsen burner.

**6** a Underline the sentence that contains a noun clause.

What I think doesn't matter.

My opinion does not matter.

b Underline the sentence that contains an adjectival clause.

My worthless opinion does not matter.

My opinion, which you have described as worthless, does not matter.

c Underline the sentence that contains an adverbial clause.

I sought his opinion because of his reputation.

I sought his opinion because he was regarded as a leader in his field.

d Underline the sentence that contains a noun clause.

I know that you are opposed to change.

I know your views about change.

e Underline the sentence that contains an adjectival clause.

Your views on change are known to all of us.

Your views, which must change, are known to all of us.

**f** Underline the sentence that contains an adverbial clause.

After you have heard my presentation, you will change your views.

After my presentation, you will change your views.

**7** Underline the subordinate clause in each of the following sentences and write in the space provided whether it is a *noun clause*, an *adjectival clause* or an *adverbial clause*.

**a** His career as a cricketer ended prematurely because he did not recover from a severe shoulder injury. ______________________________

**b** I always thought that he was a great cricketer. ______________________________

**c** His fans, who came from many different countries, were deeply saddened by his retirement.

______________________________

**d** When his autobiography was published, it was an instant bestseller.

______________________________

**8** Write *simple, compound, complex* or *compound–complex* after each sentence to describe it.

**a** Domestic cats are threatening world fish supplies. ____________________

**b** Much cat food is made from fish such as sardines, herrings and anchovies, which are an essential part of the marine food chain. ____________________

**c** Scientists estimate that almost two and a half million tonnes of such fish are used by the pet food industry. ____________________

**d** If these little fish, which are called forage fish, are overfished, larger fish such as tuna and swordfish will also be endangered. ____________________

**e** These forage fish could be used to feed people in poorer nations, but the pet food industry can pay higher prices. ____________________

**f** Pet food could be manufactured from the waste of the fish filleting industry and forage fish could then be used as human food, if countries could agree to legislate about the use of forage fish as pet food. ____________________

**9** Give examples of three types of texts where an informal style is appropriate.

______________________________

______________________________

**10** The language choices we make vary depending on our audience, purpose and context. Those choices affect the level of formality of a text. After each of the language features below, write whether it would be found in a formal or informal text.

**a** The use of contractions such as *didn't* or *can't*____________________

**b** The use of long, complex words derived from Latin and Greek ____________________ c The use of the first-person pronoun ____________________

d Fragmented or incomplete sentences ____________________

e The use of slang ____________________

**11** Write six adjectives that you could use to describe the tone of a text.

______________________________________________________________

______________________________________________________________

**12** For each of the following sentences, choose the best answer from the alternatives given. Underline your choice.

a 'She should strike while the iron is hot' is an example of:

i formal language
ii cliché
iii slang
iv simile

b 'He has been playing like an old woman' is an example of:

i discriminatory language
ii formal language
iii metaphor
iv personification

c The words 'taught/taut/tort' are examples of:

i the use of slang
ii homophones
iii adjectives
iv verbosity

d In printed text you use italics for:

i the title of a book
ii the title of a poem
iii the official title of an important person
iv capital cities

e A subjective point of view:

i is based on factual evidence
ii reflects personal opinions and feelings
iii contains a subject and a verb
iv is an example of a formal style of writing

f The connotation of a word:

i is a form of cliché
ii refers to the associations that a word can arouse, both positive and negative
iii should be avoided in formal writing
iv is an example of a synonym